Effective Altruism

For my children, Sean and Claire, and for all children of the world, today and tomorrow.

May we provide you with fulfilling lives in the present and shape a better future for you to inherit.

Effective Altruism
An Introduction

Jacob Bauer

polity

Copyright © Jacob Bauer 2025

The right of Jacob Bauer to be identified as Author of this Work has been asserted in accordance with the UK Copyright, Designs and Patents Act 1988.

First published in 2025 by Polity Press

Polity Press
65 Bridge Street
Cambridge CB2 1UR, UK

Polity Press
111 River Street
Hoboken, NJ 07030, USA

All rights reserved. Except for the quotation of short passages for the purpose of criticism and review, no part of this publication may be reproduced, stored in a retrieval system or transmitted, in any form or by any means, electronic, mechanical, photocopying, recording or otherwise, without the prior permission of the publisher.

ISBN-13: 978-1-5095-6243-5
ISBN-13: 978-1-5095-6244-2 (pb)

A catalogue record for this book is available from the British Library.

Library of Congress Control Number: 2024937090

Typeset in 11 on 13pt Sabon
by Fakenham Prepress Solutions, Fakenham, Norfolk NR21 8NL
Printed and bound in Great Britain by CPI Group (UK) Ltd, Croydon

The publisher has used its best endeavours to ensure that the URLs for external websites referred to in this book are correct and active at the time of going to press. However, the publisher has no responsibility for the websites and can make no guarantee that a site will remain live or that the content is or will remain appropriate.

Every effort has been made to trace all copyright holders, but if any have been overlooked the publisher will be pleased to include any necessary credits in any subsequent reprint or edition.

For further information on Polity, visit our website:
politybooks.com

Contents

Boxes, Figures, and Tables	vi
Introduction: What is Effective Altruism?	1
1 The Urgency of Effective Altruism: Pandemics and Prioritization	7
2 Global Poverty: You CAN Make a Difference	30
3 Weighing Uncertainties: Should You Be Vegan?	61
4 Systemic Change and Moral Pitfalls: Combating Climate Change	87
5 Can Your Career Save the World? Nuclear Weapons and Existential Risk	112
6 High Risks and Rewards: AI and Longtermism	138
7 Making a Difference through Effective Altruism	168
Notes	191
Index	213

Boxes, Figures, and Tables

Boxes

3.1	Expected value in practice: Does a pescatarian diet do more harm than good?	78
6.1	Nick Bostrom's urn of invention	141
6.2	Do future people matter? A time capsule thought experiment	146

Figures

0.1	Effective altruism symbol	2
1.1	The death toll of the pandemic compared to terrorism	12
1.2	Average $ spent on pandemic prevention per year (USA)	13
2.1	Daily preventable child deaths	32
2.2	Global income distribution	34
2.3	Average salary (USA)	42
2.4	Percentage of world population living in poverty	55
3.1	Livestock slaughtered for meat each year	65
4.1	The price of electricity from new power plants	96
4.2	Average annual greenhouse gas emissions per person (2021)	107

Tables

2.1 Peter Singer's giving scale 53
3.1 Reduction of animal products by weight 76

Introduction: What is Effective Altruism?

Every year, millions of children die from preventable and curable diseases. Natural disasters such as forest fires, droughts, and hurricanes increase in number and intensity due to climate change. Warfare is waged across the globe, contributing to a seemingly unending refugee crisis. Heightened tensions among world powers increase the risk of nuclear conflict. Countless forms of inequality and discrimination persist across the globe. The rapid development of artificial intelligence leaves our future on uncertain ground. These issues, among many others, are urgent. The world undoubtedly faces immense problems. Lives are at stake, now and in the future. The longer humanity takes to address global issues, the more lives will be lost.

It is easy to feel overwhelmed and helpless by the sheer number of challenges the world faces. It may seem impossible to make a meaningful difference in a world that is constantly in crisis. What can we do when the problems we face are so numerous and so large? Effective altruism is a movement that takes this question seriously. As the world faces increasingly complex problems, it is more important than ever to have frameworks for determining where to focus our efforts and resources. Effective altruism offers ways to do just that, using evidence and rational arguments to identify pressing issues and effective ways of solving them.

Effective altruism is a movement gaining traction in the global community, attracting a wide range of individuals, from young people who want to make a difference, to billionaire philanthropists. Though the movement is relatively young, effective altruism has mobilized thousands of individuals to work on pressing problems and has directed billions of dollars toward high-impact charitable giving. It is a diverse community composed of researchers, philanthropists, practitioners, and organizers. Effective altruists work together to find the best ways to address the world's problems and put them into practice.[1]

The movement adopted a symbol, a lightbulb with a heart filament. The effective altruism logo represents the combination of altruistic feelings, the desire to help others, and the use of intelligence to act effectively on those feelings to make a difference. Effective altruists aim to use evidence and rational argumentation to discover and support the best ways to make a large positive impact on the world.

Figure 0.1: Effective altruism symbol, Centre for Effective Altruism
Source: This logo belongs to Effective Ventures Foundation (UK), a registered charity in England and Wales with charity registration number 1149828. Used with permission.

Introduction

The name "effective altruism" was chosen in 2011 through a series of votes to describe an emerging movement of individuals devoted to improving the world as effectively as possible. Many of the movement's early founders were students from the University of Oxford, including William MacAskill, Toby Ord, Michelle Hutchinson, Holly Morgan, Benjamin Todd, and many more.[2] The movement started relatively small, with the founding of just a few nonprofits devoted to charity evaluation and high-impact career advice.[3] In a short amount of time, the effective altruism community has grown significantly. Today, it includes more than 300 organizations that have collectively mobilized billions of dollars toward researching and implementing effective solutions to world problems.[4]

After more than a decade of research, movement building, and organizational funding, what lessons does the effective altruism community have for those who aspire to improve the world? This book aims to introduce readers to the key ideas of effective altruism by exploring a range of pressing global issues and the ways in which effective altruists address them. Along the way, we'll survey important effective altruist concepts, common objections to them, and the ways effective altruists respond to those criticisms. This book is meant to help readers obtain a broad understanding of effective altruism as a movement and collection of ideas. Each chapter explores key ideas from the effective altruism movement through common cause areas that effective altruists tend to focus on. These cause areas include the following:

- *Pandemic prevention*: Preventing future pandemics and being better prepared for when they do occur could save millions to billions of lives. Modern life has raised the risk of global pandemics. In Chapter 1, we'll use the recent memory of the COVID-19 pandemic to understand effective altruism's emphasis on prioritization, and introduce the scale, neglectedness, and solvability (SNS) framework, which can help us assign our limited time and resources.

- *Health and development of the global poor*: Hundreds of millions of people live in extreme poverty, suffering from preventable diseases and ailments. There are many charities working to aid those in extreme poverty in a variety of ways, such as direct cash transfers, disease prevention, and curing blindness. Chapter 2 will explore this cause area and introduce core effective altruist concepts such as high-impact giving, charity evaluation, and cost-effectiveness.
- *Animal welfare and factory farming*: The vast majority of meat consumed comes from factory farms, where billions of land animals live in horrendous conditions. However, there is significant disagreement concerning both how much we should care about animals and what we can do to help. Chapter 3 explores this cause area as a way to introduce conceptual tools that effective altruists use to grapple with uncertainty, including expected value theory and moral uncertainty reasoning.
- *Climate change*: Climate change contributes to extreme weather events, famine, and ecosystem destruction. It has received substantial attention and resources, but many neglected interventions could use more support. Chapter 4 will explore this cause area to introduce how some effective altruist organizations emphasize systemic change as the most effective path to solving world problems. Supporting organizations that innovate and expand effective and scalable green technologies, as well as organizations that have a successful track record advocating for better governmental policies, can make a huge difference.
- *Nuclear war prevention*: Even a relatively small nuclear weapons exchange could result in a nuclear winter threatening human civilization. Attention and resources dedicated to nuclear risk have decreased since the end of the Cold War. Chapter 5 will explore this global problem as a way to introduce key effective altruist concepts related to high-impact careers and existential risk reduction. Although it is difficult to make progress in this problem area, in part due to the complexities of international relations, it can

be made through various means, especially through career paths such as research, communications, building organizations, and governmental policy work.
- *Risks from artificial intelligence*: As the power of AI technology grows, so do the risks of societal harm due to misuse, unintended consequences, and weaponization. The rapid advancement of AI could have far-reaching consequences for all those alive today and for all future generations. Chapter 6 will explore this topic alongside the effective altruist movement called "longtermism," which emphasizes the importance of positively shaping our long-term future.
- *Improving decision-making*: This diverse problem area includes improving individual and institutional decision-making on significant issues such as resource prioritization, risk reduction, making a positive impact, and evidence assessment. Given the complexity of global problems, improvements in decision-making can lead to faster overall progress on a broad range of issues. While each chapter introduces conceptual tools meant to help improve decision-making, Chapter 7 summarizes some of these ideas and frameworks from the effective altruism movement and gives practical tips on how to implement them in your life.

By exploring effective altruist concepts alongside the diverse cause areas they work on, this book aims to provide readers with a comprehensive introduction to the effective altruism movement and provide useful conceptual tools for making a positive impact on the world.

Solving the world's biggest problems requires more than just hope and goodwill. Effective altruists look to reason and evidence to find where people can make the most substantial and enduring impact. Whether or not you are part of the effective altruism community, the frameworks, tools, and concepts that it develops could help you to better understand global problems and what can be done about them. The hope for this book is that by learning from the concepts, arguments, and frameworks of the effective altruism movement, as well as objections to them, readers will be better equipped with a diverse set of tools to build a better world. Through studying movements like effective altruism, we have the opportunity to work toward a future where the immense problems we face today become a distant memory.

Progress requires dedicated time and resources. Next, in Chapter 1, we will explore the problem of pandemics, drawing upon the example of the COVID-19 pandemic and the ethical challenges of medical triage to highlight the need to prioritize our limited time and resources. We will dig into its implications and how effective altruism offers insights and approaches to tackling the prioritization of our world problems.

1

The Urgency of Effective Altruism: Pandemics and Prioritization

How can we make a difference in a world full of problems? With so many urgent issues across the globe, individuals cannot address everything. We only have a finite amount of time and money available. According to effective altruists, to have the greatest impact on the world, an important step is to identify the most pressing problems and determine how we can best utilize our limited time and resources to help solve them.

As we will see, effective altruists propose a conceptual tool to help with prioritization: the SNS framework, which evaluates problems based on their scale, neglectedness, and solvability. This is a core concept for the effective altruism movement. Understanding this framework is key to understanding effective altruism more broadly. In this chapter, we use our recent shared global experience of pandemics to explore effective altruism's advice on how to prioritize the problems we face. First, we'll explore how medical triage during the COVID-19 pandemic can help us understand the need to evaluate our options and focus our efforts on the best ways we can help others.

1.1 Pandemics and the world in triage

We all became acutely aware of the necessity of prioritization throughout the COVID-19 pandemic. Early in the pandemic, the world looked on in horror as hospitals in Italy were overrun with patients. Rooms grew scarce, and essential medical equipment dwindled. Medical professionals faced gut-wrenching decisions on whom to admit to hospital beds, whom to prioritize, and whom to provide the limited available medical resources.[1] One doctor described the harrowing process as "deciding who is eligible for intensive care, who to let go, and who to treat with intermediate devices."[2] To address this challenge, an Italian professional medical society published triage guidelines that prioritized "patients with the highest chance of therapeutic success," considering factors such as age, health conditions, and chances of survival.[3] Unfortunately, this traumatic scenario repeated across the globe as countless hospitals grappled with the same life-or-death decisions. As resources became increasingly scarce, difficult decisions had to be made on how to use those resources to help those in need.

Throughout the COVID-19 pandemic, governments and medical organizations issued special triage guidelines to manage the unprecedented stress on healthcare systems. Triage is not unique to pandemics; it is an everyday occurrence in hospitals and emergency rooms worldwide. Within healthcare systems, triage is a commonly used practice to assess patients based on the severity and treatability of their conditions, determining the order of priority for medical care. While various triage systems and guidelines exist, according to the National Library of Medicine, they share a universal goal "to supply effective and prioritized care to patients while optimizing resource usage and timing."[4] The simple reason triage was common practice throughout the pandemic, and an everyday occurrence throughout healthcare systems, is that it saves lives.

To help illustrate the need for prioritized care, consider the following simplified example. Suppose you are in charge of a hospital at the height of a pandemic. Your hospital has a maximum of 100 beds available, but due to a COVID outbreak in your community, 1,000 people are requesting to be admitted with a range of severe symptoms. Many of the patients will survive without your assistance, though the hospital could help them recover quicker. Some, unfortunately, are too far gone for any hospital treatment to save them, though it could keep them alive for a few more hours or days. Others, however, will survive only with the service your hospital can provide. Although they all could benefit from treatment, your hospital cannot help all of them. If you tried to admit everyone, your resources would be stretched too thin to be much help to anyone; you would also put your medical professionals at extreme risk of infection and burnout, making them less able to help those who come to the hospital in the future.

Perhaps you could admit people on a strictly first-come, first-served basis; whoever is at the front of the line gets a bed if available. However, this all but guarantees that many of the beds will be taken up by those you cannot save and those who would be okay without your help. As a result, many of the people who need treatment the most won't get it.

What if you admit people based on severity alone? In this case, you risk only treating those who cannot be saved, while those you could help most are turned away. In order to save the most lives, healthcare professionals look for indicators that can help them prioritize patients based on factors such as severity, urgency, and treatability to determine who will be admitted first and who will have to wait or be turned away. Even for those who are treatable and have severe cases, further prioritization can help better allocate resources. Some people may need immediate attention; for others, treatment might be necessary, but they will be okay if they receive it later.

Triage systems involve some of the most difficult decisions individuals can face, and these systems are not perfect. Although medical professionals do their best to rely on evidence-backed indicators, there is no way to know for certain who is in the most need of care. Some of the people you turn away might die, and some of the people you treat may have survived without your help. Nonetheless, triage gives those with the most urgent, life-threatening, treatable conditions a far higher probability of receiving timely and efficient care. Without triage systems prioritizing care, far more people would die in hospitals every day and potentially millions more would have died during the pandemic.

The COVID-19 pandemic underscored the importance of assessing the urgency and nature of treatment for individuals in order to allocate limited resources effectively. Triage, in essence, involves prioritization to better utilize limited resources. The fundamental principles of triage were widely employed throughout the pandemic. Prioritization was crucial not only in hospitals but also in the distribution of personal protective equipment, such as N-95 masks, and the rollout of vaccines. Medical professionals and the most vulnerable populations were often given priority in receiving protective equipment, vaccines, and the newest medical treatments as they were developed.

At present, the world finds itself in a situation similar to overrun hospitals during the COVID-19 pandemic – faced with many great needs but limited resources. There is only so much each of us can do. We, as individuals, have limited time, resources, and attention that we can dedicate. We can imagine our available time and resources, which we want to use to help the world, as beds in a hospital. Thousands of patients are at the door, each representing different problems to which we could devote our resources, but there are far too many for us to meaningfully help them all.

Triage provides a framework for approaching the innumerable global problems that humanity faces. Just as medical professionals employed imperfect triage methods throughout the pandemic to achieve better overall outcomes, effective altruism suggests adopting similar approaches to our efforts in addressing world problems.

With countless global issues competing for our attention, the effective altruism movement emphasizes the need to prioritize and allocate resources thoughtfully. Otherwise, we risk spreading our resources too thin or missing opportunities to prevent unnecessary suffering. While applying triage principles to global problems may be imperfect, akin to the imperfections of hospital triage, the hope is that embracing this mindset will lead to better prioritization of our time and resources, enabling us to make a more significant difference in the world. As we'll explore next, just as hospitals prioritize patients with diverse ailments based on factors like severity, urgency, and treatability, effective altruists propose a similar framework to prioritize the problems we face to better focus our resources.

1.2 Prioritizing global issues: The SNS framework

Effective altruists use a shared general framework for prioritizing global problems. This framework comes in many variations sharing similar fundamental principles.[5] The version we'll explore is the scale, neglectedness, and solvability (SNS) framework:[6]

- *Scale* (also called importance): How big is the problem?
- *Neglectedness* (also called crowdedness): How much attention and resources are currently directed toward addressing the problem?
- *Solvability* (also called tractability): Will allocating additional resources likely lead to new solutions or expand existing ones?

These factors provide valuable insights for comparing and prioritizing world problems. They are meant as a starting point in exploring ways to improve the allocation of our limited resources. Let's examine each of these three factors in more detail.

The first factor, scale, weighs the size of the problem, especially in comparison to other global issues. When considering the scale of a problem, some key questions to explore include:

- *Extent*: How many individuals are affected by the problem?
- *Intensity*: How significant is the problem for those affected?
- *Duration*: How long-lasting are the issues for those affected?[7]

For instance, while stubbing one's toe may happen to billions of individuals annually and cause intense pain, the duration is usually momentary. On the other hand, terrorism impacts far fewer people, but the intensity is far more severe, resulting in roughly 480,000 deaths since 1970.[8] Needless to say, the duration of the effects of terrorism is far greater compared to stubbed toes. This is not to imply that we should disregard efforts to prevent stubbed toes or design products to minimize such suffering. Rather, it emphasizes that preventing terrorism is a much more substantial global problem.

While the scale of terrorism is significant, how does it compare to the scale of pandemics? In terms of impact on individuals, both terrorism and pandemics can result in death or lifelong disability, with comparable intensity and duration. Pandemics are much less frequent than acts of terrorism; however, pandemics affect a much larger number of people when they do occur. Terrorism has claimed around half a million lives over a span of fifty years, whereas the COVID-19 pandemic claimed more than 20 million lives in less than four years.[9]

Although the extent of pandemics far surpasses that of terrorism, the intensity and duration for those affected are

Figure 1.1: The death toll of the pandemic compared to terrorism
Sources: Author's figure based on data from *The Economist*, "The Pandemic's True Death Toll"; START, "Global Terrorism Database 1970–2020 [Data File]."

similar in both. This does not imply that efforts to prevent terrorism should be disregarded – terrorism is unquestionably a significant issue. However, considering our limited time and resources, the SNS framework suggests that, all else being equal, preventing pandemics should receive greater overall resources than preventing terrorism, given their respective scales.

While scale is an important consideration, it is possible for a problem of large scale to already receive substantial funding and research. This leads us to the next factor in the SNS framework: neglectedness. Neglectedness examines whether an appropriate amount of resources is allocated to a problem in relation to its scale. In general, the more neglected an area is, the greater the potential impact of devoting resources to it. Assuming two problems are equally important, channeling more resources toward the more neglected problem is likely to yield a greater impact.

In the case of preventing pandemics versus counter-terrorism, the United States, for example, spends an estimated $8 billion per year on the former compared to $280 billion per year on the latter.[10] This suggests that pandemics are relatively neglected in terms of US spending compared to counterterrorism. It is an indicator that increasing spending

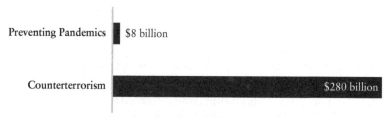

Figure 1.2: Average $ spent on pandemic prevention per year (USA)
Source: Author's figure based on estimates from the Centre for Effective Altruism, "What Is Effective Altruism?" (n.d.). The annual estimates were derived using data from C. Watson et al., "Federal Funding for Health Security in FY2019," *Health Security* 16 (October 17, 2018); N. Crawford, "The U.S. Budgetary Costs of the Post-9/11 Wars through FY2022" (2022), https://watson.brown.edu/costsofwar/figures/2021/BudgetaryCosts.

on preventing pandemics would likely do more good than increasing spending on counterterrorism. While both problems are important, the SNS framework suggests that preventing pandemics should be given higher priority due to its larger scale and greater neglectedness.

Neglectedness is sometimes referred to as "crowdedness," reflecting the idea that too many resources allocated to a particular area can diminish the benefits gained. This is a well-known concept within economics called the law of diminishing returns, which states that the benefits per resource often decrease as more resources are allocated to a project. As time, research, and resources are dedicated to a problem, the easiest approaches to address that problem are usually explored first. As more effort is invested, the readily available solutions become exhausted or already operate at full capacity. As a result, only the more challenging aspects remain, requiring significantly more time and resources to resolve. This does not imply that investing one's time or money in a problem that already receives considerable attention will have no positive effects. However, as a general rule, such contributions are likely to have a relatively smaller impact compared to areas with fewer resources dedicated to them. It is also possible to search for neglected areas within a specific problem. Even if a particular problem is already crowded and well funded, there may be overlooked approaches to address the issue.

With neglectedness, the SNS framework suggests seeking out overlooked problems or underdeveloped approaches to problem-solving. This is sometimes referred to as "low-hanging fruit." Fruit closer to the ground on a tree are easier to pick, but as those lower fruits are collected, what remains on the tree becomes increasingly difficult to harvest. Devoting resources to neglected problems, which still have low-hanging fruit, often results in a greater overall impact. Neglectedness is an indicator that low-hanging fruit remains; there could be easy solutions that just need more attention and resources to bring to fruition.

To help identify neglected problems, the following are some helpful questions to consider:

- Is the problem widely known, or are people largely unaware of it?
- Is the problem infrequent but large in scale when it occurs?
- Are the individuals affected by the problem often overlooked?[11]

These questions serve as useful indicators of neglectedness. Issues that receive substantial press coverage often already have numerous resources devoted to them relative to the size of the problem. Some large problems go unnoticed due to their infrequency, despite their immense impact. For example, prior to COVID-19, experts had long warned about the world's lack of preparedness for a large-scale pandemic. However, since pandemics occur infrequently, it is challenging to sustain attention and mobilize resources in advance. In the decade preceding the COVID-19 pandemic, funding for pandemic prevention and preparedness by the Centers for Disease Control and Prevention (CDC) decreased.[12]

Sometimes, large problems are overlooked because they affect individuals who are out of sight and out of mind. When new diseases start spreading in foreign countries, it can be difficult to mobilize a sufficient international response to help combat the threat until the pathogen starts affecting people closer to home. In 2019, the USA cut funding to PREDICT, a pandemic-prevention program aimed at detecting and monitoring viruses globally.[13] However, emergency funding was issued to the program after COVID-19 began to impact the USA in 2020.[14]

A problem might be well known and receive substantial resources, yet, due to its scale, it can still be neglected. Although COVID-19 has drawn attention and resources to the issue of pandemics, many effective altruists still view pandemic preparedness and biosecurity as neglected problem areas because of the overall scale of suffering and death they can cause. Many claim that there is much more that we can do to prevent the next pandemic, which leads us to the third factor of the SNS framework: solvability.

Solvability, also referred to as tractability, emphasizes the notion that allocating the same amount of resources to two different problems may not result in the same level of progress, even if the problems are of equal scale and neglectedness. When evaluating world problems, effective altruists ask how feasible it is to make progress on each problem. Some problems are inherently more challenging to solve than others, requiring significantly more resources to achieve the same amount of progress.

One way to assess solvability is to think about the level of resources needed to make significant progress in addressing a problem. While this estimation can be challenging, asking the following questions can provide insights into solvability:

- Are there existing solutions that can be expanded?
- Are there promising avenues of research for developing solutions?
- Is there a realistic chance of a breakthrough advancement with a massive impact?[15]

Some problems already have solutions; they just need additional resources to expand the delivery of them. For instance, low-cost surgery can cure individuals with blindness caused by cataracts, yet millions of people with vision impairments from cataracts lack access to this cure.[16] In some cases, solutions or treatments might not exist yet, but there is high confidence that research efforts will eventually yield results. For example, early in the COVID-19 pandemic, numerous vaccine development efforts received substantial funding with the expectation that at least some of them would result in effective and safe vaccines. Additionally, during the pandemic, significant advances were made in pathogen detection in community wastewater, which could be developed into an early detection tool in future pandemic prevention and mitigation. Some problems might be extremely difficult to solve, such as preventing future pandemics, but investing in promising research is still worthwhile given the potentially massive impact if a breakthrough is achieved.

Overall, applying the SNS framework to the cause area of pandemic prevention and preparedness could result in something like the following:

- *Scale*: Pandemics happen on an immense scale, with COVID-19 alone causing millions of deaths. Bioterrorism, bioweapons, and lab leaks of engineered pathogens pose immense risks as well. In worst-case scenarios, engineered pandemics could wipe out most or even all of humanity.
- *Neglectedness*: Much more attention and resources have been directed toward pandemic prevention and preparedness since the COVID-19 pandemic, but given the scale of the issue, it could still be considered relatively neglected. As memories of COVID-19 become more distant, it may be difficult to maintain or increase the level of resources needed.
- *Solvability*: There are existing and developing technologies that show promise in reducing risks in this problem area. Other avenues for progress include policy change, research, mitigation strategy, and advocacy to maintain and grow biosecurity.

This gives us a way to compare this cause area with others and puts us in a better position to explore how we can utilize our time and resources.

Some versions of the SNS framework include an additional factor: personal fit.[17] When considering how to devote your time or career to benefiting the world, it makes sense to prioritize based on your personal talents, skills, opportunities, and passions. By carefully evaluating your personal fit alongside what is needed to help solve world problems, you can better direct your efforts to make a greater difference. In addition to scale, neglectedness, and solvability, personal fit requires reflecting on your unique set of characteristics to determine which problem you are best suited to help solve (more on this in Chapter 5).

Having gained an understanding of the SNS framework, let's now explore what problems effective altruists tend to prioritize as the most pressing, given their scale, neglectedness, and solvability.

1.3 The world's most pressing problems

Effective altruists tend to categorize the world's most pressing problems into three main groups: global poverty, animal welfare, and global catastrophic risks.[18] Using the SNS framework, let's explore why.

Global poverty is large in scale, relatively neglected, and extremely solvable. More than 600 million people live in extreme poverty, often lacking access to essential medical care, sanitation, and nutrition. The problems of those living in extreme poverty receive less attention compared to individuals in wealthier nations. As a result, thousands of people die each day from preventable causes. This highlights why many effective altruists work on problems related to global poverty. We already have developed cures for many of the problems faced by the global poor. Those cures just aren't reaching those who need them most. By directing resources to organizations that work to make essential cures and treatments more accessible and affordable for the most impoverished communities, you can make a huge difference in the lives of others. (We'll explore this topic more in Chapter 2.)

Effective altruists tend to see the problem of animal welfare, or animal suffering, as large in scale, extremely neglected, and highly solvable. This might be the most controversial cause area that effective altruists work on. Whether you view it as one of the most pressing world problems will depend on your views on whether animal suffering matters and by how much. (We'll explore this topic more in Chapter 3.) However, as long as you care about the lives of animals to some degree, it is easy to see why many effective altruists prioritize animal welfare. More than 100 billion land animals live in terrible conditions in factory farms, and trillions of wild animals are affected by issues such as habitat destruction. The suffering of other species is often overlooked, especially if it isn't visible. As such, the problems related to animal welfare tend to be extremely neglected in comparison to other world problems. Nonetheless, solutions are possible, and promising work is being done, especially in the area of reducing animal suffering in factory farms through changing regulations, reducing meat demand, and creating meat alternatives.

The broadest category includes global catastrophic risks, which have the potential to result in immense harm. Effective altruists highlight numerous global catastrophic risks, including pandemics, climate change, nuclear warfare, and advanced artificial intelligence. Each risk in this category will have differing results using the SNS framework. Overall, by their very nature, catastrophic global risks have the largest possible scale. Given that they are often rare and hard to predict, they tend to be relatively neglected in relation to their scale, but, at the same time, developing solutions to prevent them can be extremely difficult. While the ever-developing power of human technology has led to immense benefits for humanity, it also increasingly creates a multitude of catastrophic risks that threaten the world. Some effective altruists see this rate of increased risks as unsustainable and, as a result, view catastrophic risk reduction as the highest priority cause area, requiring far more time and resources to find solutions before it is too late.

The categories of global poverty, animal welfare, and catastrophic risks are just an overview of the global problems that effective altruists tend to prioritize. It is not comprehensive. The effective altruism movement is broader than these, with individuals working on diverse problem areas such as strengthening democracies, mental health, criminal justice reform, and improving decision-making. Effective altruists continually debate what problems deserve the highest priority. Furthermore, many effective altruists also work on lower-priority problems when they think that, in addressing them, they are particularly well suited to have a significant impact. This ongoing debate and the recognition that individuals can make significant contributions to various causes have fostered a diverse community of people working together to address the numerous challenges our world faces in many different ways.

Now that we have surveyed the high-priority problem areas within the effective altruism community, which are the results of applying the SNS framework, let's examine the objections and limitations to this framework, which play an important role in shaping the movement's approach to cause selection.

1.4 Objections and limitations to the SNS framework

The SNS framework is a tool for thinking about global priorities, but, like any tool, it has its share of limitations and objections that should be considered. Concerns raised about the SNS framework have shed light on important concepts, contributing to the ongoing development of global priorities research. Specifically, three key objections worth noting relate to the potential oversight of important problems, quantification bias, and the inherent uncertainty involved in evaluating each factor of the SNS framework. Let's explore each of these and the ways effective altruists can respond to them.

The first objection arises from the results produced by the SNS framework, indirectly raising questions about its validity. Many people consider problems such as discrimination, inequality, immigration crises, biodiversity loss, and curing cancer to be of utmost importance. However, these issues often receive lower priority within the cause areas identified by effective altruist organizations using the SNS framework. If the SNS framework has major flaws in the results it produces, underprioritizing important problems, it suggests flaws in the framework itself.

One way effective altruists can respond to this objection is by arguing that there are good reasons why certain problems are not ranked as high priority using the SNS framework. Those problems might simply rank too low in terms of scale, neglectedness, and/or solvability. Some problems may be urgent and significant at an individual or community level, but their scale is not large enough to register as high priority in a global context. Alternatively, certain important issues might already be receiving considerable attention and resources relative to other large-scale problems; in other words, they are not neglected issues. Moreover, there are instances where addressing a large-scale problem proves exceptionally challenging, even with additional resources devoted to it. These considerations do not imply that lower-priority problems should be ignored. Rather, they indicate that other problems are in more immediate need of additional global attention and resources.

While taking these reasons into consideration, many critics argue that the current priorities of the effective altruism movement are still too narrow, advocating for the inclusion of numerous other pressing issues as high priority. Additionally, many object to some of the cause areas that effective altruists focus on, such as animal welfare or catastrophic risk, arguing that they are overprioritized. If the results of the SNS framework are erroneous, it could be due to flaws in the framework itself. One possible flaw in the framework is a common objection to the overall approach of effective altruism: quantification bias.

Quantification bias is the overemphasis on quantifiable metrics, resulting in important aspects that are more difficult to measure being overlooked. Since a central part of the SNS framework is evaluating the scale of the problem, it can easily lead to focusing too heavily on issues that are more easily quantified. As a result, critics claim that the SNS framework overlooks or discounts important issues while overprioritizing others. For example, Emma Marris claims that "effective altruism discounts the ethical dimensions of relationships, the rich braid of elements that make up a 'good life,' and the moral worth of a species or a wetland."[19] These ethical dimensions, and many others, are difficult to measure or quantify. Even if we could quantify them, it is difficult or impossible to compare them to other ethical dimensions; this is sometimes called the problem of incommensurable goods. For example, how should you weigh the saving of an animal species from extinction against distributing life-saving vaccines? The dangers of quantification bias and the problems associated with the difficulty of comparing certain types of world problems lead some to conclude that the SNS framework is flawed, or, at the very least, limited in what it can tell us about world problems.

One way effective altruists respond to these objections is to acknowledge the concerns and emphasize the need for ongoing global priorities research. Rather than considering it definitive or exhaustive, effective altruists can view the SNS framework as one useful tool among others that will hopefully be developed in the future. This approach has led to the establishment of organizations such as the Global Priorities Institute and Rethink Priorities, dedicated to further investigation of global problem prioritization. But even with extensive research, blind spots can persist, resulting in the overlooking of important and urgent problems and cause areas. Recognizing this, effective altruists sometimes use the term "Cause X" to refer to problem areas that the movement currently severely overlooks or underprioritizes.[20] Identifying Cause X and improving global priorities research are considered important cause areas by many effective altruists, to the extent that they consider them among the most pressing problems to work on.[21] As more rigorous research is conducted and more conceptual tools are developed, lists of the highest-priority global problems should grow and evolve.

Another significant set of challenges for the SNS framework involves the high levels of uncertainty when assessing the scale, neglectedness, and solvability of global problems. The sheer size and complexity of these problems make accurate assessments challenging. For instance, determining what constitutes significant harm often involves subjective value judgments, leading to variations in the assessment of the scale of problems. As a result, while the SNS framework is widely used within the effective altruism movement, effective altruist organizations and individuals reach different conclusions regarding problem prioritization.

One point of disagreement within the effective altruism community is how much weight to give to scale as opposed to solvability, which has led to the emergence of two general camps within the movement: longtermists and neartermists. Longtermists focus on problems that affect future generations, considering the scale of the consequences for the long-term future. These problems tend to be much larger in scale but also far more difficult to solve, given the inherent uncertainties in predicting the far future and the complexity of the issues involved (see Chapter 6 for more on longtermism). Neartermists, on the other hand, focus on problems facing individuals alive today or in the near future, which are still significant in scale but lack the multiplier effect of including individuals from the far future. The solutions to current problems are often clearer and more tangible than those of the distant future, making them more appealing to neartermists. Many effective altruists, however, fall somewhere in between, recognizing the importance and neglectedness of both long-term and near-term global problems. Nonetheless, this debate within effective altruism underscores the challenges of grappling with uncertainty when applying the SNS framework to complex global problems.

The challenges surrounding the SNS framework are akin to debates concerning hospital triage, where prioritizing patients based on symptoms to determine urgency and treatability also involves significant uncertainty. However, having a framework, even an imperfect one, for prioritizing patient care can result in better resource allocation and ultimately save more lives. Over the years, patient triage methods have continuously adapted and improved, incorporating new research findings and technologies to better prioritize patient care. Similarly, effective altruists hope that a comparable iterative approach will be taken in the global prioritization of world problems. In the meantime, some uncertainties can be mitigated by treating the SNS framework as an informal starting point for prioritizing global problems, providing valuable indications that warrant further research, hard work, and exploration.

1.5 Solutions are possible: Preventing future pandemics

Throughout this chapter, we've explored the devastating impact of pandemics as a way to introduce the importance of prioritizing global problems using the SNS framework, a core effective altruist concept. By considering the scale, neglectedness, and solvability of various issues, effective altruists identified pandemic prevention as a top priority long before the emergence of COVID-19. The immense scale of death and suffering caused by pandemics, as demonstrated by the COVID-19 global crisis, underscores the need for proactive measures to prevent future outbreaks.

Pandemic prevention remains a top cause area for many effective altruist organizations. While this cause area has received increased attention since the outbreak of the COVID-19 pandemic, it is still far from being solved. Moreover, the resources devoted to it are still small compared to its scale. To put it into perspective, the COVID-19 pandemic alone claimed around the same number of lives in the USA as all American deaths from wars since 1775, an estimated 1 to 1.4 million lives lost (based on excess mortality calculations).[22] While preventing wars is an important priority in its own right given the immense scale of death and suffering involved, the SNS framework suggests that preventing future pandemics should also be given high priority.

Another reason why pandemics are a high-priority problem is that they may become more frequent and severe in the future unless we take preventive measures. Experts warn that many aspects of modern civilization increase the risk of future global pandemics, underscoring the urgency of addressing this problem area. These risk factors include:

- Increasing global interconnectedness, which makes it easier for novel pathogens to spread rapidly across borders and continents.[23]
- Modern meat production, which increases pandemic risks in many ways, such as increasing contact with wild animals by encroaching on natural habitats and providing high-density animal populations for novel pathogens to propagate; this increases the chances of diseases jumping to humans (a process called zoonosis).[24]
- Some forms of well-intended pathogen research increase the risk of accidental lab-originating pandemics, such as gain-of-function (GOF) research, which involves modifying pathogens to increase their transmissibility or virulence, in order to study how they evolve and how to treat them.[25] Accidental release or misuse of engineered pathogens could result in even worse pandemics than naturally occurring ones.[26]

Failing to address the increasing risk factors for pandemics could result in future catastrophic pandemics far worse than what we experienced with COVID-19.

Fortunately, there are organizations working on addressing these issues related to pandemics through research, innovation, and policy change. One such example is the Johns Hopkins Center for Health Security, which conducts research and advocacy on topics such as biosecurity, biosafety, outbreak detection, and response. As the risks of pandemics increase, the need for resources to support these types of efforts also rises. By donating to, working for, or raising awareness about such organizations, individuals can support the crucial work of preventing future pandemics.[27]

With so many pressing global challenges, such as preventing pandemics, it is important to recognize that no single person can shoulder the burden of solving them alone, but it is also important to recognize that solutions are possible and progress is being made toward finding them. For example, we witnessed during the COVID-19 pandemic the collective efforts made by individuals, organizations, and governments, all of which played a vital role in combating the crisis. We can all contribute to finding solutions to the world's most pressing problems in many different ways, whether through our careers, our monetary support, or our political advocacy. In this chapter, we have learned that we can use the SNS framework as a tool to compare and prioritize different problems based on their scale, neglectedness, and solvability. This framework can help us identify where our limited resources can make the most difference and how we can be part of the solution. The history of humanity is filled with remarkable transformations when people unite to tackle common problems. Assessing the scale, neglectedness, and solvability of problems can help us identify the best ways that we can contribute to finding and implementing solutions.

Not all problems are equally important or equally neglected. Some problems are more urgent and more solvable than others. In this chapter, we have explored how effective altruism uses the SNS framework to prioritize global problems. In the next chapter, we will explore one problem that effective altruists are best known for highlighting: global poverty. The problem is immense but far from hopeless. We will see how effective altruism can help us navigate this problem and how we can make a difference.

Questions for reflection

1. What global problems do you find the most important or urgent? Why?
2. Choose two global problems and compare them using

the SNS framework. How do these factors influence your assessment of their importance and potential for impact?
3. Are there any problem areas that you believe are currently overlooked or underprioritized? Provide reasons or evidence to support your perspective.
4. Reflecting on the SNS framework, evaluate its effectiveness in prioritizing global problems. Discuss both its strengths and limitations, and consider what factors you would remove or add. Explain your reasoning.
5. Reflecting on the global response to the COVID-19 pandemic, how do you think it reflects the prioritization of pandemic prevention as a global problem? What could have been done differently then, and what could be done differently now to better address this issue?
6. Based on what you have learned about effective altruism and its approach to global problems, how might you adjust your thinking or actions to make a positive impact in the world? Explain your reasons.

Classroom exercise

Imagine you have $1 billion to allocate exclusively toward addressing world problems. How would you distribute this funding? Explain why. What criteria or considerations guide your decision-making process?

Helpful resources

Introducing and defining effective altruism

"What Is Effective Altruism?" *Centre for Effective Altruism.* https://effectivealtruism.org/articles/introduction-to-effective-altruism.

William MacAskill, "The Definition of Effective Altruism," in Hilary Greaves and Theron Pummer, eds., *Effective Altruism: Philosophical Issues*. Oxford: Oxford University Press, 2019, pp. 10–28.

Jacob Bauer, "What's Effective Altruism? A Philosopher Explains," *The Conversation*, 2023. https://theconversation.com/whats-effective-altruism-a-philosopher-explains-197856.

The SNS framework (also called ITN framework)

Robert Wiblin, "A Framework for Comparing Global Problems in Terms of Expected Impact," 80,000 Hours, 2016. https://80000hours.org/articles/problem-framework/.

Benjamin Todd, "Want to Do Good? Here's How to Choose an Area to Focus On," in *80,000 Hours: Find a Fulfilling Career that Does Good*. Oxford: Trojan House, 2023, Ch. 4. https://80000hours.org/career-guide/most-pressing-problems.

"Analyzing Cause Areas," Probably Good. https://probablygood.org/career-guide/analyzing-cause-areas.

William MacAskill, "Poverty vs Climate Change Versus ... Which Causes are Most Important?" in *Doing Good Better: How Effective Altruism Can Help You Make a Difference*. New York: Gotham Books, 2015, Ch. 10.

Global priorities research

Roman Duda, "Global Priorities Research," 80,000 Hours, June 2023. https://80000hours.org/problem-profiles/global-priorities-research.

"A Research Agenda for the Global Priorities Institute." https://globalprioritiesinstitute.org/research-agenda.

Pandemic preparedness and biosecurity

"Improving Biosecurity and Pandemic Preparedness," Giving What We Can. https://givingwhatwecan.org/cause-areas/long-term-future/biosecurity.
Arden Koehler and Benjamin Hilton, "Preventing Catastrophic Pandemics," 80,000 Hours. https://80000hours.org/problem-profiles/preventing-catastrophic-pandemics.
Toby Ord, "Pandemics," in *The Precipice: Existential Risk and the Future of Humanity*. New York: Hachette Books, 2020, pp. 124–37.

2

Global Poverty: You CAN Make a Difference

Each year, millions of people die from preventable causes. The majority of these deaths are children in low-income countries. Lacking access to the basic necessities of life leads to immense suffering for the hundreds of millions of people who live in extreme poverty. Many of the ailments afflicting those living in poverty are ones for which we have already developed cures and effective interventions. Thankfully, there are many charities working on expanding access to evidence-backed solutions to those who need them most. By identifying and donating to the most impactful charities, we have the ability to expand access to these life-saving solutions, helping the most underprivileged people in the world.

This chapter explores the nature of extreme global poverty and our unique ability to make a difference. It shows how effective altruists suggest that we can be part of the solution by directing a portion of our income to high-impact charities. Even modest donations, when directed to the right organizations, can cure blindness, prevent deaths from treatable diseases, or even double a family's annual income. Looking for the best ways to alleviate global poverty is at the heart of the origins of effective altruism and helps explain foundational effective altruist ideas.

Key concepts we will explore include charity evaluation, cost-effectiveness, moral arguments for giving, and a strategy called "earning to give." The chapter also grapples with challenging questions. Do charities sometimes do more harm than good? How much are we morally obligated to donate? As we'll see, while the effective altruism community actively debates these issues, there are rigorous, evidence-backed ways in which we can each make a profound difference in the lives of others. But first, let's explore the scale of suffering from extreme poverty in our world and why many readers of this book might be in a unique position to help.

2.1 Wealth: One of our superpowers

For those around the globe living in poverty, the consequences are dire. Poverty, especially extreme poverty, often results in a lack of access to necessary medical care, nutrition, education, and sanitation facilities. A heartbreaking consequence of this is that children are far more likely to die from preventable causes before reaching adulthood. Every year, globally, 5.9 million children die. The vast majority of these deaths are from preventable causes in lower-income countries. The youth mortality rate in low-income countries is 8.1 percent compared to only 0.6 percent in high-income countries (per 100 live births).[1] Parents on a higher income have more access to the basic necessities of life, including life-saving treatments for their children. Of the 5.9 million children who die every year, more than 5 million of them would be saved if the global child mortality rate were reduced to that of high-income countries.[2] This gives us a sense of how many child deaths are preventable: nearly 14,000 each day. This is equivalent to forty-six jumbo jet crashes every single day, each carrying only children.[3] Figure 2.1 illustrates this shocking reality. The sheer scale of this preventable loss of young lives is hard to grasp, yet it is the daily reality for thousands of families.

The origins of effective altruism involve grappling with our privileged global position and how best to use that privilege

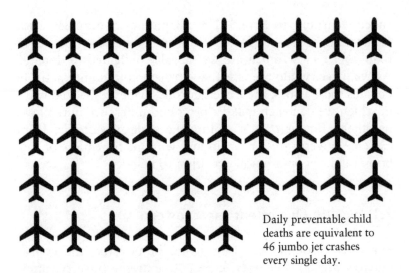

Daily preventable child deaths are equivalent to 46 jumbo jet crashes every single day.

Figure 2.1: Daily preventable child deaths
Source: Author's calculations using data from *Our World in Data*, "Youth Mortality Rate" (2023), and Aviation Safety Network, "100 Worst Aviation Accidents," n.d.

to help the most underprivileged people in the world. Many people living in modern industrialized countries may not realize that they are among the wealthiest individuals globally, and that with that wealth comes the ability to use resources to cure terrible ailments and save the lives of those living in extreme poverty. Readers of this book likely are, or will be, among the world's wealthiest people. We may not feel wealthy compared to others around us in our communities. But those of us able to routinely purchase books, take vacations, eat out at restaurants, purchase over-the-counter medicine, and obtain higher education stand far above the vast majority of our fellow humans in terms of living standards and economic means. Even a modest income in the European Union or the United States represents almost unimaginable fortune to billions struggling in poverty.

More than 6.5 billion people, 85 percent of the world's population, live on less than $11,000 per year, well below the US national poverty line.[4] The global median annual income is less than $2,600, meaning the majority of people on earth live on less than $50 each week.[5] More than 600 million people live in extreme poverty, on less than $785 per year.[6] These numbers are adjusted to have similar purchasing power to the same amount of dollars in the United States. Imagine trying to pay for your weekly groceries and medicines with only $15 or less. This is an everyday reality for hundreds of millions of people living on less than $2.15 a day, the international poverty line in 2023. In contrast, the median annual income of someone in the United States who has a bachelor's degree is around $74,000, more than $200 a day.[7] The graph in Figure 2.2 depicts the global income distribution. Where do you fall on this graph? If you are a student, where do you expect to fall on this graph once you become settled into your future career? If you make $30,000 per year, you will be among the wealthiest 3 percent of people in the world. If you make more than $60,000, you will be in the top 1 percent.

The wealth of individuals living in high-income countries can be seen as a superpower, giving them heightened abilities compared to most of the world. It provides individuals with easy access to the basic necessities of life and to the cures of many deadly diseases that afflict millions of people in low-income countries. In our interconnected world, our wealth also gives us the power to help those in extreme poverty, for example by donating to charities that increase access to essential resources and interventions to those that desperately need them. There are tangible ways that everyday individuals with high incomes, by global standards, can help the global poor in immense ways, saving lives and curing ailments. One of the most effective ways is by donating to charities that directly help the global poor. However, there are countless charities to pick from. For those who want to help prevent some of the thousands of lives that are needlessly lost each day, how can we best use our resources to do so?

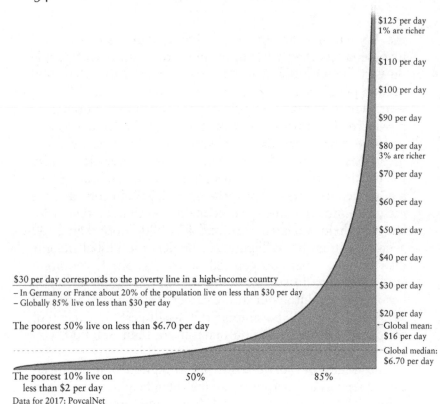

Figure 2.2: Global income distribution
Source: Author's figure adapted from Max Roser, "Global Economic Inequality: What Matters Most for Your Living Conditions Is Not Who You Are, but Where You Are," *Our World in Data* (2021).

*Differences in the cost of living between countries are taken into account Incomes are adjusted and expressed in international-$

2.2 Origins of effective altruism: High-impact charities

In 2009, two years before the term "effective altruism" was coined, a pivotal moment in the development of the movement took place when Oxford philosophers Toby Ord and William MacAskill launched Giving What We Can, an organization aimed at inspiring people to channel their charitable contributions toward evidence-backed interventions that have the greatest impact in aiding the global poor. But what evidence was there on which charities and what programs actually helped people the most? Two years earlier, a group of friends were asking similar questions. They decided to investigate, believing sound evidence must exist on which programs actually help people the most. However, what they found was that traditional charity evaluators focused on metrics like overhead costs and CEO pay, not the impact of donated funds. Seeking better data, in 2007 Holden Karnofsky and Elie Hassenfeld founded GiveWell, a nonprofit committed to finding the best charities and sharing transparent analysis on the impact per dollar donated on the lives of others.[8]

Ord and MacAskill's organization, Giving What We Can, built directly on GiveWell's principles and research on evidence-based giving. To this day, in partnership with GiveWell's research, Giving What We Can recommends high-impact charities with the goal of catalyzing a community devoted to evidence-based effective giving. Within a year of its founding, Giving What We Can had sixty-four members, pledging an impressive $21 million in donations. By 2023, the organization had grown to more than 9,000 members, who have pledged to give over $3 billion to charity, with over $200 million already donated.[9]

Through careful research and analysis of evidence, charity evaluators have revealed that people's donations can have an astonishing impact when they are targeted toward the most effective charities. What can a donation to the highest-impact charities actually do? A donation to The Fred Hollows Foundation of as little as $50 can cure a person of blindness. Protecting an individual from iodine deficiency, which can lead to terrible health effects such as brain damage, costs as little as $0.10 per year through the Iodine Global Network. Expanding deworming programs costs around $0.50 per treatment and expanding access to safe drinking water costs around $1.50 per person per year through the charity Evidence Action.[10]

Donations from a single individual can provide effective and transformative resources to those who would not otherwise have access to them. A charity that embodies this principle is GiveDirectly, which provides direct cash transfers to those living in extreme poverty. GiveDirectly identifies recipients subsisting on less than $2.15 per day and directly transfers cash to them via mobile payments, allowing them to spend it however they wish to improve their lives. After taking into account organizational and delivery costs, around $0.83 of every dollar donated to GiveDirectly is transferred to the global poor. As a result, donating $80 a month is enough to more than double a person's income; donating $40 a month is enough to lift a person out of extreme poverty. Recipients typically use the funds they receive to purchase basic necessities like food, medicine, clean water, tin roofs, and school fees. GiveDirectly's model reflects the immense impact donations can achieve when targeting the poorest individuals globally.

Direct cash transfers are seen as a baseline for how much good can be done for individuals through donations. GiveDirectly was listed as a top charity by GiveWell and Giving What We Can until relatively recently; since then, some other charities have had an even higher impact per dollar by targeting specific interventions. GiveDirectly's cash transfer program is still highly praised; GiveWell now uses it as a benchmark to which other charities are compared.[11] In 2022, GiveWell updated its top charity criteria to only include those that are at least ten times as cost-effective as those of GiveDirectly.[12] As of writing, GiveWell's and Giving What We Can's top charities include:

- Malaria Consortium: Malaria is one of the leading causes of child mortality in low-income countries. It is a life-threatening disease that affects more than 200 million people each year, primarily in low-income countries, resulting in more than 600,000 deaths. Around $7 protects a child from malaria through antimalarial drugs, with an estimated cost-effectiveness of $5,000 per life saved.

- Against Malaria Foundation: Malaria is caused by a parasite that mosquitoes pass to humans. Bed-nets protect people from mosquito bites while sleeping, thereby reducing transmission rates. Around $5 provides one bed-net that protects multiple people from malaria transmission from mosquitoes for years. This program has an estimated cost-effectiveness of $5,500 per life saved.
- Helen Keller International: Vitamin A supplements help prevent blindness and strengthen immune systems. It's estimated that more than 200,000 children die each year due to vitamin A deficiencies. Around $1 delivers a vitamin A supplement, reducing child mortality. This program has an estimated cost-effectiveness of $3,500 per life saved.
- New Incentives: Nigeria has the second highest child mortality rate globally. New Incentives provides conditional cash transfers to incentivize parents to bring their babies to clinics for routine vaccinations, which reduces child mortality. Around $160 vaccinates an infant who would not otherwise have been protected, with an estimated cost-effectiveness of $5,000 per life saved.[13]

Each of these charities has high estimated cost-effectiveness backed by strong evidence of impact through things like monitoring programs and randomized control trials. Although Helen Keller International has the best estimated cost-effectiveness backed by strong studies, GiveWell ranks the Malaria Consortium and the Against Malaria Foundation higher on their top charities list due to their having exceptionally strong evidence of impact from many high-quality studies.

The immense good that can be achieved through donations to effective charities illustrates how even modest sums by global standards can be life-changing for those in extreme poverty. The research on cost-effective interventions indicates that it takes as little as $3,500 on average to save one life through donations. This possibility of doing so much good has inspired many effective altruists to give large portions of their income to high-impact charities. Notably, the philosopher Peter Singer views donating large portions of one's earnings as an ethical obligation in light of the enormous positive impact these donations can have on people in dire situations. The origins of the effective altruism community began with charity evaluation, but the moral inspiration for this work came from Singer's arguments concerning our ethical obligations to donate. The next section will introduce Singer's influential pond analogy and explore the moral conclusions he derives from it.

2.3 Moral inspiration of effective altruism: Singer's pond analogy

Although effective altruism is less than two decades old, the moral inspiration for the movement dates back to 1971 with philosopher Peter Singer's seminal essay "Famine, Affluence, and Morality." In this essay, Singer first articulated his influential arguments for the moral obligation to donate to charities that help those suffering from poverty, famine, and disease. He claimed that we should prevent terrible things from happening if we can do so without making a comparable sacrifice. In some cases, we have positive moral obligations – duties to act or intervene to help others.

To illustrate this point, Singer shared a thought experiment called the pond analogy. Imagine walking past a shallow pond and seeing a drowning child. You could easily save the child, but doing so would muddy your nice clothes. Singer argues that any decent person would save the child. A child's life holds far more moral significance than ruining one's shoes or clothing. Singer concludes that if we can prevent something bad without sacrificing anything of moral significance, we ought to do it.

Singer extends this principle to donating to charity. He claims that the pond example is analogous to those of us living in affluent countries with extra money to spend on luxuries. Like the drowning child, there are people in extreme poverty who will die or suffer curable diseases without intervention. We can't sacrifice our clothes to physically pull them to safety, but we can sacrifice the money we would use to buy extra, unnecessary clothing to donate to effective charities providing life-saving resources to those who would not otherwise have them. Donating money requires little sacrifice relative to the moral significance of saving a life. As such, Singer argues that we have an obligation to donate substantially to effective charities. He concludes that, since we have the ability to make a difference, we have the same moral obligation to help those who are suffering from poverty, famine, or disease in distant parts of the world as we do to help those who are suffering nearby. It doesn't matter how far away from you a person in need is; what matters is whether or not you can help.

Singer's pond analogy is an illustration of his core moral argument, which can be summarized as follows:

Premise 1: If we are able to prevent something bad from happening without sacrificing anything of comparable moral significance, we ought to do it.

Premise 2: It takes very little money to save or dramatically improve the lives of those in extreme poverty (e.g. providing interventions such as bed-nets, deworming, or cash transfers).

Conclusion: Therefore, we ought to donate our extra money to save or dramatically improve the lives of those in extreme poverty.

Singer uses the term "comparable moral significance" to capture the idea that we should only sacrifice something if it is of equal or greater moral significance than what we are preventing. For instance, the argument does not imply that we should donate if it means risking our own lives or that of our loved ones. However, it does imply that we should donate if it simply means giving up some luxuries or comforts that are not essential for our wellbeing for the sake of preventing terrible things from happening to others. For most people in affluent countries, this argument implies that we should be giving away the money we would normally spend on luxuries, a majority of our income, since it could be saving lives and curing terrible diseases if directed toward high-impact charities.

For most people, Singer's conclusion is too morally demanding, setting the standards of an ethical life too high. Do we really have such a strong moral obligation to give so much of our money away? The main avenues to critique Singer's core argument are to deny or add qualifications to premises 1 or 2. For example, perhaps there are some limits to how much we can reasonably be expected to sacrifice for the sake of others. In the pond example, if there are thousands of ponds, each with a drowning child, you can only save so many children before you risk your own life in exhaustion.[14] Some critique premise 2 by casting doubt on the effectiveness of charitable giving, claiming that it could lead to more harm than good. We'll explore these objections and more later in the chapter. However, it is difficult to completely whittle down the argument to the point that we have no obligation to give to high-impact charities. Even if most charities are harmful, it is difficult to see how all of them would be. Even if there are thousands of ponds with drowning children in them every day, and you cannot be expected to save all of them, deciding to save none seems wrong. It still seems reasonable that you should budget some time to save some lives if you have the ability to do so with limited sacrifice of your own time and money. There is a lot of room between the positions of giving nothing and giving everything to high-impact charities.

Effective altruists come to differing conclusions on whether we have a moral obligation to give to high-impact charities. For many, Singer's argument is their inspiration to become effective altruists, looking for the most high-impact charities to give the majority of their wealth. For others, Singer's arguments are a call to action but set a baseline of the good you can do in the world. At a minimum, you could donate enough to high-impact charities to save or dramatically improve the lives of many people living in some of the most underprivileged places in the world. However, there are many other ways that you could use your time and resources to make an even bigger impact on the world. Furthermore, not everyone living in affluent countries will be in a position to give substantial amounts of their money due to factors such as unstable employment, costly health or family obligations, and/or high amounts of debt.

Although there is disagreement among effective altruists on how far we should take the implications of Singer's moral argument, this core argument does nonetheless shape a common outlook among effective altruists. It has inspired millions in donations with the view that charitable giving is more than just a nice thing to do, it is a moral duty (to some degree). To do otherwise would be akin to walking by that shallow pond, allowing the child to die for the sake of your clothing. Singer's arguments for the moral obligation of giving have had an immense impact on effective altruism, influencing many of the movement's founders, including Toby Ord and William MacAskill, who credit Singer's work as one of the inspirations for founding Giving What We Can.

We live in a world where everyday people in affluent countries do remarkable things to help the most underprivileged people in the world, simply by clicking a few buttons and giving up some luxuries. Next, we'll explore one of the most well-known concepts from the effective altruism movement, which can be seen as a natural implication of Singer's argument – the practice of earning to give. If the more money you donate to effective charities, the more lives you can save, then, by seeking higher-paying jobs, you could save more lives with that extra income.

2.4 Earning to give

The basic strategy of earning to give is to earn more money so that you have more to give away. Earning to give is the concept of making as much money as you can, often by pursuing high-paying careers, in order to donate large portions of that income to effective charities.

Most ethical frameworks emphasize helping others in need. Earning to give is one way to enact the virtues of charity, beneficence, and compassion on a larger scale. Rather than working directly for a charity, someone might have a job in business, finance, technology, or some other field so as to maximize their income. They then donate large portions of their salary, perhaps 50 percent or more, to thoroughly vetted charities. These charities can use the funds to save lives from treatable diseases, reduce poverty, or enact other highly effective interventions. MacAskill presents three main reasons in support of earning to give: discrepancy in earnings, making a difference, and effectiveness of charities. Let's go over each of these.

First, high-paying careers provide substantially more disposable income that could be donated compared to lower-paying careers. High-paying careers can enable one to donate far more over one's lifetime compared to nonprofit charity work. Even donating a fraction of a high salary can surpass donating the majority of a lower salary. For example, at the time of writing, the average salary of a finance manager in the USA is $166,000, whereas the average salary for working in community and social service occupations is $55,800.[15] Working as a finance manager, and donating a third of your salary, would still leave you with almost double the income

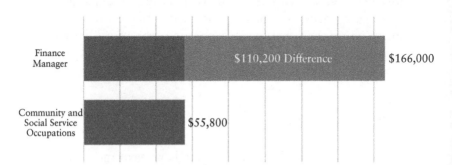

Figure 2.3: Average salary (USA)
Source: Author's figure based on data from Bureau of Labor Statistics, "May 2022 National Occupational Employment and Wage Estimates" (April 25, 2023).

of someone working in a social service job – in fact, you could donate more than $100,000 a year and still have more income. Over the course of your career, this could result in millions of additional dollars directed to charity.

MacAskill's second reason in favor of earning to give is the concept of making a difference, which is sometimes referred to as assessing the counterfactual. If you want to improve the world, your actions should lead to more good compared to what would have happened otherwise. To illustrate this point, MacAskill gives the following example:

> Suppose you come across a woman who's had a heart attack. Luckily, someone trained in CPR is keeping her alive until the ambulance arrives. But you also know CPR. Should you push this other person out of the way and take over? The answer is obviously "no." You wouldn't be a hero; you wouldn't have made a difference.[16]

This basic idea also applies to the charity sector. Charities are often people-rich, but money-poor. They often have plenty of applicants for their open positions, but require more funding to expand services.[17] MacAskill argues that taking a high-paying job likely won't decrease the number of people entering lower-paying charity careers, as others will readily fill any open positions, doing about as good a job as you would have done in that role. However, taking a high-paying job and donating significantly to effective charities probably would make a difference, as most people donate very little, only around 2 percent of their income.[18] If you didn't take that job, someone else would. But by earning more and giving more, you would likely donate significantly more than the other person would have done in that professional position.

The third reason MacAskill gives is the effectiveness of high-impact charities. As explored earlier in the chapter, certain high-impact charities can save lives and cure diseases with relatively small amounts of money. The more funding these charities receive, the more resources they can provide for the most impoverished people in the world. You don't have to be a millionaire to make a difference, but the more money you make, the more money you can give. Using GiveWell's cost-effectiveness estimates, giving 10 percent of a six-figure salary would save multiple people's lives when directed to the right charity. A finance manager giving 50 percent of their salary to high-impact charities could save the lives of fifteen to twenty-three people each year, all while still having more income to live on compared to working in the charity sector directly. This example illustrates the potential impact of earning to give; however, earning to give does not necessarily mean pursuing the highest-paying job in the business sector to maximize wealth and thereby donations. It could simply mean seeking promotions or finding a well-compensated, satisfying job in order to donate more than you otherwise would have.

MacAskill concludes that earning to give is a powerful way of doing good, especially for those who have access to jobs that are among the highest paying in the world. While we should all choose our careers carefully and take more than just earning potential into account, the amount of good we can do with a higher income provides strong evidence for the merits of earning to give. For those who want to do good with their careers, earning to give is a compelling option worth considering. This argument exemplifies effective altruism's emphasis on exploring ways to do the most good possible, even when it leads to unconventional conclusions.

So far in this chapter, we have explored some of the most well-known concepts born of the effective altruism movement, including charity impact evaluation, moral arguments for giving, and earning to give. These are also some of the most heavily criticized effective altruist concepts. In the remaining sections of this chapter, we will explore some of the key objections raised against effective altruist approaches to giving and how proponents of effective altruism respond to such criticisms.

2.5 Objections: Does giving do more harm than good?

Effective altruism's goal is to help others, but some critics contend that it causes more harm than good with its giving recommendations. Let's examine three of these common objections: (1) the potential harms of high-earning careers, (2) the negative consequences of charitable aid to communities, and (3) the potential harm to high-income economies from giving too much. These objections raise important questions about the potential unintended consequences of well-meaning efforts to make a positive impact. We will explore each objection in detail and consider how effective altruists respond to them.

The first objection focuses on earning to give, claiming that many high-paying jobs, such as careers in finance, are harmful to society. This objection challenges the idea that you can do good by earning a lot of money and donating it to effective charities if the source of your money is morally questionable. A high-profile example of this is the FTX and Sam Bankman-Fried scandal.

Inspired by effective altruism, Sam Bankman-Fried decided to work in finance and cryptocurrency to make as much money as he could so that he would have more to give to high-impact charities. At the beginning of 2022, it seemed that he had achieved this goal, with Forbes valuing his net worth at more than $26 billion thanks to his cryptocurrency exchange company FTX and trading firm Alameda Research.[19] Bankman-Fried pledged to give billions of dollars away to effective causes and had already donated millions. In 2021, he founded the FTX Foundation, which gave $160 million in philanthropic grants. He was highlighted as a success story by many effective altruist organizations, showing just how much good one person can do through earning to give.

However, by the end of 2022, in a series of scandals, Bankman-Fried's wealth all but evaporated alongside billions of his customers' funds. This led to his arrest and eventual conviction of fraud. Almost overnight, he went from being a symbol of the high-impact potential for the earning to give strategy to a cautionary tale that emphasized the need for careful consideration of the impacts of career choices. This case highlights the concern that effective altruist advice on charitable giving can lead to more harm than good, even if you start out with good intentions.

One way that effective altruists respond to this objection is by stating that Sam Bankman-Fried was not following the advice of leading effective altruist organizations. Long before the FTX scandal, the most well-known effective altruist organization that promotes earning to give as a strategy for doing good, 80,000 Hours, advised against pursuing careers that cause harm, even if the aim is to offset the damage through high-impact donations. For example, in an article published in 2017, 80,000 Hours advocated avoiding harmful high-paying careers, even if you think your donations would do more good, for four main reasons: (1) It might violate rights, (2) you are probably wrong about the benefits and/or harms involved, especially due to hidden harms, (3) moral caution and uncertainty (we'll explore these concepts more in Chapter 3), and (4) there are better alternatives.[20]

Overall, the advice from effective altruists is that if you believe a certain career significantly harms the world, it is best to avoid it. For those interested in earning to give, there are many well-compensated careers that are beneficial to society. For example, many of the highest-paid professions in the USA are in the fields of medicine and engineering. While there is disagreement on whether finance/cryptocurrency careers are inherently harmful, effective altruist organizations advocated against performing immoral acts, like fraud, in order to donate more to charity. As a general rule, the ends do not justify the harmful means. Nonetheless, this objection and the FTX scandal highlight the dangers of rationalizing harmful acts for the sake of the greater good; it is a potential moral hazard for those using effective altruist frameworks. Earning to give requires careful consideration of the ethical implications of one's career choice.

Another common objection is that charitable aid might provide short-term benefits to the recipient but end up doing long-term harm to their communities by making them overly reliant on handouts from abroad. This objection questions the sustainability and empowerment of aid interventions and suggests that they might undermine the development of robust local systems, businesses, and grassroots solutions.

Often, the way effective altruists respond to this type of objection is to take it seriously and even highlight the concern, all while advocating for ways to do good rather than harm with donations. Effective altruists often point to PlayPumps installed across parts of Africa as an example of an aid intervention that failed, and even caused harm. PlayPumps are water pumps designed as merry-go-rounds, pumping water to a storage tank and powered by children at play. This seemed like an innovative way to provide clean water to impoverished communities. However, investigations found the pumps were problematic in a variety of ways. Compared to the standard hand pumps they often replace, PlayPumps were far more expensive, frequently broke down, and sometimes caused injuries. Furthermore, the spinning play component was often unsuitable for the needs of the communities they were meant to benefit, making it more difficult, rather than easier, for adults to pump water.[21] Despite the good intentions, the PlayPumps often made water access worse for local communities. But just because some charities are inefficient or harmful doesn't mean that they all are. Effective altruists often use this example to highlight the importance of evidence-based evaluation of the impact of charities in order to identify those that are truly improving the world.

Nonetheless, critics such as Larry Temkin argue that even well-intentioned, evidence-based aid might have unforeseeable negative long-term consequences.[22] Acknowledging this issue, charity evaluators like GiveWell investigate both short-term and long-term impacts when assessing the programs of charities.[23] Effective aid interventions can empower communities by increasing people's health and resources, allowing them to better participate in their local relationships and economies. Although it is never possible to know with absolute certainty the overall impacts of any charity, rigorous research can help estimate results and reduce uncertainty. This type of objection highlights the need for careful consideration of the long-term effects of different interventions in order to reduce the possibility of unintended harm.

A third common objection is that if everyone gave in the way that effective altruists suggest, this would lead to a worse world, as the economies of high-income countries would suffer or even collapse. This objection raises a macro-level economic concern about the consequences of reduced consumer spending in affluent nations.

Peter Singer's response to this type of objection is that we don't currently live in a world where most people will give in this way anytime soon.[24] As noted earlier in this chapter, only around 2 percent of income in the United States goes to charity. Since current average levels of giving are so low and are not expected to increase in the near future, the negative impacts on high-income economies are negligible, whereas the measurable positive impacts on people living in extreme poverty are significant.

Even if we lived in a world where people gave so much to charity that we started seeing large negative effects on local economies, an advantage of earning to give is its flexibility to changing circumstances such as this. If it turns out that evidence shows that your money will do more good locally than abroad, you can easily divert your giving. Effective altruists aim to help others as much as possible based on the best available data. As such, they often readily adapt their giving if new information reveals better ways to help others. Both GiveWell and Giving What We Can recommend researcher-managed giving funds that regularly update where donations go based on the best available evidence.[25] However, this does not mean that reduced consumer spending has no drawbacks. It is best to acknowledge these possible trade-offs but weigh them against the benefits of helping others in extreme poverty or suffering.

Overall, the objections in this section help to show that donating is not a simple or straightforward decision, but rather requires careful consideration of the overall impacts of giving. These objections raise important issues for effective altruists to consider, and highlight the importance of considering whether a charity's programs result in more harm than good. Assuming that at least some charities are truly high-impact, doing immense good with the funds they receive, a natural question arises: How much should we give? The next section explores this question alongside related objections.

2.6 Objections: How much to give?

Another common objection to effective altruism's general approach is that giving a high percentage of your income to charity is unsustainable on a personal level; people are not likely to stick with it. For example, if you take a high-paying job in order to give more to charity, you are also likely to be influenced by the living standards of your peers and feel tempted to spend more on yourself. Alternatively, giving such a large portion of your income while working at a demanding job could lead to burnout, which could result in you losing your job or just deciding to no longer give in the future, thinking that you have done enough already. How can one overcome these challenges and sustain a high level of giving over time?

One way effective altruists respond to this objection is to acknowledge the difficulty but offer advice on ways that can make it easier. For example, Giving What We Can gives several recommendations. First, they recommend joining communities of like-minded givers either online or in person. Engaging with communities in this way can help foster and maintain your motivation and commitment to giving, as well as give you a sense of meaning and belonging. Additionally, you could keep track of the estimated good that your donations have done, which can also give you a sense of meaning and joy. Giving What We Can offers resources to do both on their website.

Another way to help you maintain your level of giving is by taking a public giving pledge, which can have the added benefit of inspiring others. Giving What We Can currently recommends three different giving pledges:

- *The Pledge*: A public commitment to give at least 10 percent of your income to high-impact effective charities. This is their main pledge, and more than 8,000 people have taken it.
- *The Trial Pledge*: A smaller version of the main pledge, a public commitment to give a specified amount, 1 percent or more, to effective charities for a chosen period of time. After the trial period ends, you have the option to extend the pledge time period, increase the pledge amount, or simply end the trial. More than 4,000 people have taken this pledge.
- *The Further Pledge*: A public commitment to give all income above a chosen amount to effective charities (and to give at least 10 percent of your income). This chosen amount is adjusted each year with inflation. Giving What We Can does not publish the number of Further Pledges taken; however, both Toby Ord and William MacAskill have taken this pledge. They both live on less than $35,000 a year, donating any additional income to high-impact charities.[26]

The goal of these public pledges is to increase the accountability of givers, helping them stick to their values and maintain their giving level, as well as encourage others to give.[27]

Given Singer's moral arguments on the duty of giving, how much should individuals commit to donating? Perhaps the most salient objection to the effective altruist approach to giving is that it is too demanding. If we follow Singer's pond analogy to its logical conclusion, it seems that we should be donating all the money that we would normally spend on luxuries in order to help those living in extreme poverty. The objection claims that this is excessive self-sacrifice. Although many people would admire donating in such a fashion and consider it to be morally praiseworthy, akin to monks and nuns who take vows of poverty, they would not consider it morally obligatory. This objection argues that people have a right to enjoy their hard-earned money and that a moral duty to give everything away would be too harsh and unrealistic. Making such excessive demands could turn some people away from giving altogether, as they might feel the notion is too outlandish to consider seriously.

Luke Freeman, executive director of Giving What We Can, warns against all-or-nothing giving; he calls such approaches the "extremes of giving."[28] He agrees that giving away everything you possibly can is excessive for most people and risks leading to burnout, in which case the giver and the people who could have been helped in the future are worse off. However, giving nothing misses immense opportunities to help others. Nonetheless, even these extreme approaches might be right for some people. Some people have very little to give and need to focus on their immediate needs; others, such as students, are focusing on building skills now in order to be able to better benefit the world in the future. On the other side of things, some saintly figures are able to live lives of near voluntary poverty, giving away all their excess money. Most people, however, fall somewhere in between these two extremes.

Freeman recommends considering other more moderate giving standards that might be a better match. These standards align with the giving pledges offered by Giving What We Can. If we find ourselves agreeing with Singer, that we have a strong moral obligation to give substantial amounts to charity, a better approach might be to pick a living standard that we can live with comfortably and sustainably, and then give away the extra money we make beyond that. That way, we could still enjoy an affluent lifestyle by global standards, while doing an immense amount of good. Freeman calls this the "give what you don't need" standard for giving.[29]

Another standard for giving is to give generously. What exactly counts as generous is ambiguous. It could mean giving far more than the average of 2 percent. In some religions the standard is 2.5 percent of wealth each year (zakat) or 10 percent of your income (tithing). The main pledge promoted by Giving What We Can also sets the standard at 10 percent, since this is more generous than what most people give and easier to calculate than estimating total wealth.

Another possible giving standard is giving what you won't miss. This approach aligns with Giving What You Can's trial pledge, which starts at 1 percent of income. Given the pond analogy argument, this may come as a surprise, but this is the giving standard that Peter Singer recommends starting with. Singer has long claimed that giving is not all or nothing, that giving some is better than giving none, and that saving some lives is better than saving no lives. However, in the tenth anniversary edition of his 2009 book *The Life You Can Save*, Singer suggests a much more modest giving scale than he did in his original writings on the topic. He now recommends giving an amount that would not create any personal hardship, which may mean as little as 1 percent of income for those making less than US$81,000 a year. He recommends giving more as you enter higher income brackets, as the amount you can give without hardship should increase as you have more income. In this way, you can live a comfortable life and still make a significant difference in the world. Singer's recommended giving scale is shown in Table 2.1 (in US dollars). He calculates that if everyone in the United States gave by these suggested donation levels, it would raise over US$600 billion in donations, more than enough to lift everyone on earth out of extreme poverty.

Peter Singer still holds that, as long as our money can do so much good in the hands of high-impact charities, the

Table 2.1: Peter Singer's giving scale

Donation Amount	Income Bracket
1% of the first $81,000	$40,000 – $81,000
5% of the next $59,000	$81,001 – $140,000
10% of the next $180,000	$140,001 – $320,000
15% of the next $160,000	$320,001 – $480,000
20% of the next $1,520,000	$480,001 – $2,000,000
25% of the next $9,000,000	$2,000,001 – $11,000,000
33.3% of the next $42,000,000	$11,000,001 – $53,000,000
50% of the remainder	Over $53,000,000

Source: Author's table adapted from Peter Singer, *The Life You Can Save: How to Do Your Part to End World Poverty*, Tenth anniversary edition (Sydney: The Life You Can Save, 2019), p. 221.

moral ideal is to donate all the money we would normally spend on luxuries. However, he also acknowledges that moral standards are often unattainable, but, nonetheless, we should not let perfection be the enemy of the good. Singer claims that by giving just 1 percent to high-impact charities, even though the moral ideal is much higher than this, we are likely to be doing far more to address global poverty than most individuals, and, as such, our donation level is morally praiseworthy. As we start giving, we can reflect each year on whether we could give more without hardship, and gradually increase our level of giving over time. It may be impossible to live a morally perfect life, but moral standards can be seen as ideals to work toward, offering ways to continually improve as individuals. However, many people note that an important part of improving as individuals is by contributing to our local communities, which leads us to the next section.

2.7 Objections: Near before far?

Another common objection to the effective altruist approach to charitable giving is that many people believe charity starts at home and that it is better to prioritize helping local communities than those far afield. They argue that although it is good to be aware of global issues, the most impact can be made nearby, where you can build relationships, have direct experience of the problems, and see what works and what doesn't. For example, they might say that volunteering at a local soup kitchen or donating to a local animal shelter is more meaningful and effective than sending money to a distant country.

Effective altruists often highlight that there is nothing wrong with helping people we know and in our communities, and that engaging with our surroundings is an important part of being human; however, that doesn't have to come at the cost of ignoring the plight of the most underprivileged people in the world. It might be true that for almost all of human history, the people we could help most were those in our local communities (this might be why we have strong intuitions for it); however, effective altruists claim that modern technology has now changed this by giving us the ability to have an immense impact on far away people across the globe.

We live in a unique time in human history. In the past, it was difficult or impossible for everyday people to help those outside their city or country. They had limited information, communication, and transportation options. Over the past 200 years, technology has transformed this. It is now possible to interact with and aid people beyond traditional borders. We can communicate with people from different cultures and backgrounds. We can access reliable information about the problems and solutions in different parts of the world. We can transfer money quickly and securely to effective charities that operate globally. Average individuals in affluent nations can save lives and cure ailments simply by clicking on a few links and diverting some of their resources. In the past, this simply was not possible. It also may not be possible in the future.

Thanks to global efforts, the world is making substantial progress in reducing poverty. As discussed at the beginning of this chapter, thousands of children still die each day from preventable causes. This is an immense tragedy. However, these deaths are not inevitable. Before the modern era, the child mortality rate was around 49 percent. This means that for most of human history, around half of all children died before adulthood. This persisted across the globe until the late 1800s, when child mortality rates began to improve steadily. By 1990, child mortality had dropped to around 10 percent globally. This progress is continuing. By 2021, this had dropped to around 4.4 percent.[30] This corresponds with a similar drastic drop in global extreme poverty rates during the same time frame. In the early 1800s, more than 75 percent of people lived in extreme poverty. By 1990, this fell to around 30 percent. Progress continues to be made, bringing the estimated number of people living in extreme poverty to around 10 percent in 2018.[31]

Some people see the steady downward trends in global poverty and child mortality as an objection to effective altruism's focus on this problem. The objection claims that, as

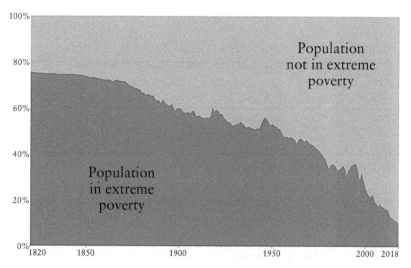

Figure 2.4: Percentage of world population living in poverty
Source: Author's figure adapted from Max Roser, "Extreme Poverty: How Far Have We Come, How Far Do We Still Have to Go?," *Our World in Data* (August 27, 2023).

global economies grow, the increased production of goods will naturally take care of the problem over time. According to this view, investing more resources into addressing global poverty is unnecessary, as economic development will take care of the issue on its own. They might point to examples of countries like China or India, claiming that these countries have lifted millions of people out of poverty through economic growth.

A possible response to this objection is that even though progress is being made, progress is not inevitable. It takes a global effort to maintain and advance progress on global issues like eliminating global poverty. Many factors could threaten or reverse the gains made so far, such as wars, diseases, and natural disasters. Many of the interventions that effective altruists promote may also help accelerate economic development, as it is much easier to be productive when you are not sick and have proper nutrition. Another response to this objection is that, even if it is true that progress is inevitable and global poverty rates will naturally continue to decrease, it doesn't address the reality that millions of people will suffer and die without intervention. Even if global extreme poverty is no longer an issue in the future, that is no solace to the hundreds of millions of people suffering in extreme poverty today. We can still work to prevent as much suffering as we can with our resources now.

2.8 More than giving to the global poor

This chapter has focused on the effective altruist approach of donating to cost-effective charities that aid those living in extreme poverty. However, it is important to acknowledge that charitable donations are not the only way to make a positive difference in the world. In this concluding section, we'll explore and respond to common objections to effective altruism based on the perception that it focuses too narrowly on philanthropy alleviating extreme poverty as the primary source of doing good. Through this discussion, we'll introduce the wider scope of careers and cause areas within contemporary effective altruism, which the remainder of the book will explore in more detail.

Some people understandably find the notion of working in high-paying professions solely to maximize donations inherently unmotivating. Feelings of fulfillment in your work are important for mental health and career satisfaction. Often people want to find work that they are passionate about or find careers that benefit others directly. While some research indicates people often can adapt to find meaning in new careers over time, strategies such as earning to give clearly do not suit everyone. However, it is also important to note that many practitioners of earning to give do find profound purpose and satisfaction in high-earning roles precisely because they enable large-scale charitable giving that tangibly helps others.

Another frequent objection to high-impact giving is that there are many other ways to have a larger positive impact on the world, and, as such, effective altruism overemphasizes donating to charity as the primary avenue for doing good. Beyond just giving to high-impact charities, other avenues like policy change, research, innovation, advocacy, or hands-on charity work may potentially do even more good in certain contexts.

Some may find it surprising that most effective altruist organizations readily acknowledge that donating money is just one high-impact option of doing good among many. For example, the effective altruist organization 80,000 Hours helped popularize earning to give as a high-impact career path. However, they estimate it only suits around 10 percent of the people they advise, acknowledging many other ways to benefit the world.[32] Earning to give suits some skill sets and personalities, but effective altruists also recognize the importance of cultivating researchers, policy analysts, charity entrepreneurs, on-the-ground activists, and more. For any complex global problem like global poverty, climate change, or pandemic preparedness, progress requires diverse talent pursuing varied approaches.

Effective altruism has expanded well beyond a narrow focus on one approach to doing good for one cause, donating to alleviate global poverty. While improving conditions for the extremely poor remains an urgent priority for the movement, effective altruists today work on a wide range of global issues, as discussed in Chapter 1, including pandemic prevention, climate change, factory farming, nuclear weapons policy, and risks from artificial intelligence. For instance, Giving What We Can now recommends high-impact charities across cause areas like animal welfare, catastrophic risk reduction, and more.

Effective altruism seeks to identify the most pressing problems facing current and future generations, determining not only the most effective interventions and policies, but also the most urgent challenges themselves. Charity evaluation is complex and continuously debated within the community. There will always be uncertainty in assessing how to do the most good given limited resources. However, effective altruism's principles aim to provide guidance for allocating time, money, and talent despite inherent difficulties in quantifying impact. The next chapter explores how effective altruists grapple with deep uncertainties in areas like animal welfare and what tools can aid decision-making even with limited information.

Questions for reflection

1. What responsibilities, if any, come with being among the world's wealthiest people in terms of ability to help the poorest people in the world? How much should those with high incomes, in a global context, give to charity? Explain.
2. Do you find Peter Singer's pond analogy convincing? What objections or concerns do you have? How do you think Singer would respond?
3. Do you think earning to give is an ethical career path? What do you think are the most compelling arguments for and against it?

4. In what ways do you think today's world enables individuals to have a greater impact on global issues compared to times in the past? Provide examples.

Classroom exercise

First, estimate the average income of individuals in your career field. Next, enter that income into Giving What We Can's online "How Rich Am I?" calculator: https://www.givingwhatwecan.org/how-rich-am-i. Next, enter 10 percent of that income into The Life You Can Save's online impact calculator: https://www.thelifeyoucansave.org/impact-calculator/. Discuss the results of each as a class or in small groups.

Helpful resources

Global extreme poverty and child mortality

Max Roser, "Extreme Poverty: How Far Have We Come, How Far Do We Still Have to Go?" *Our World in Data*, August 27, 2023. https://ourworldindata.org/extreme-poverty-in-brief.

Max Roser, "The World Is Awful. The World Is Much Better. The World Can Be Much Better," *Our World in Data*, February 2024. https://ourworldindata.org/much-better-awful-can-be-better.

High-impact charities

Luke Freeman, "How Much Money Should We Donate to Charity?" *Giving What We Can*, May 27, 2021. https://

www.givingwhatwecan.org/blog/how-much-money-should-we-donate-to-charity.

"Our Best Charities," *The Life You Can Save.* https://www.thelifeyoucansave.org/best-charities/.

"How We Produce Impact Estimates," *GiveWell*, February 2024. https://givewell.org/impact-estimates.

Peter Singer's arguments on giving

Peter Singer, "Famine, Affluence and Morality," *Giving What We Can*. This includes the full original essay (1971) along with a summary of key points and commentary. https://www.givingwhatwecan.org/get-involved/videos-books-and-essays/famine-affluence-and-morality-peter-singer.

Peter Singer, "The Argument," in *The Life You Can Save: How to Do Your Part to End World Poverty*, 10th anniversary edn. Sydney: The Life You Can Save, 2019, Ch. 1. https://www.thelifeyoucansave.org/the-book/.

Earning to give

Benjamin Todd, "Why and How to Earn to Give," *80,000 Hours*, March 2023. https://80000hours.org/articles/earning-to-give/.

Derek Thompson, "The Most Efficient Way to Save a Life," *The Atlantic*, June 15, 2015. https://www.theatlantic.com/business/archive/2015/06/what-is-the-greatest-good/395768/.

3

Weighing Uncertainties: Should You Be Vegan?

When we have imperfect information, how can we determine the best course of action? Effective altruists grapple with deep uncertainty when evaluating how to make the greatest positive impact. This chapter explores key concepts used by effective altruists to address uncertainty, including expected value theory and maximizing expected choice-worthiness. These strategies inform decision-making despite unknowns. We will apply these ideas to a case study on factory farming and veganism.

Significant uncertainty exists regarding the moral status of animals and our ability to affect their conditions. Effective altruists are ten times more likely to be vegan than the general population,[1] often claiming that veganism is an easy way to improve the world by reducing unnecessary suffering. But questions remain. Are animals conscious and capable of suffering? If so, does changing your diet meaningfully reduce the suffering of animals? Using expected value theory and maximizing expected choice-worthiness, we will explore the ethics of our diets amid uncertainties around factory-farmed animals.

First, it is important to understand the gravity of making decisions under moral uncertainty. To provide context on the high stakes of dealing with uncertainty, we will introduce an alarming concept: moral catastrophes.

3.1 Moral catastrophes

According to philosopher Evan G. Williams, moral catastrophes have three key elements: (1) they are large-scale, (2) they involve serious wrongdoing, and (3) responsibility for them is widespread.[2] History provides countless examples of moral catastrophes, from systemic and oppressive discrimination to slavery and genocide. Disturbingly, Williams argues that, just as with past civilizations, we are likely unknowingly guilty of moral catastrophes right now. He gives two arguments in support of this claim.

The first argument is what Williams calls the "inductive worry." He points to the fact that every society in history has had major moral blind spots. To illustrate this, consider the ancient Romans. They viewed themselves as an advanced civilization, yet they kept slaves and crucified dissidents. The Romans saw these acts as justified, even virtuous. Today, we view such practices as grievous moral failings. The Romans are not alone. Essentially, every other society and culture throughout history has turned out to have major moral blind spots. As such, Williams claims it stands to reason that we likely have moral blind spots too, especially given that certain moral catastrophes are in our very recent past, such as racial segregation and denial of women's right to vote.

Williams contends that, like the Romans, our society's moral standards probably fall far short of ideal ethics. In this view, future generations might well look back in horror at actions we currently applaud or accept as normal. The Romans viewed themselves as morally superior to the barbarians, as they had abolished human sacrifice.[3] Williams claims we are likely in a similar position – although we have made much moral progress compared to previous generations, there is still more progress left to be made, progress that is difficult to see when we live under current cultural standards.

The second argument put forward by Williams is the "disjunctive worry." He argues that we could be committing moral catastrophes right now due to having wrong moral beliefs on major issues. Some examples of topics that could result in moral catastrophes if we are wrong about them include such questions as: Who should count as having moral standing? When should we intervene in the choices of others? What counts as abuse? What rights should we respect? And how much consideration should we give to future generations? Williams claims that being wrong on any one of these issues, and many more, could have disastrous moral consequences. But the chances of being right on all of them are very low. As an example, he states that even if we were 95 percent confident on fifteen independent moral issues, we would still have only about a 46 percent chance of avoiding moral catastrophe ($0.95 \wedge 15 \approx 0.46$).

However, even this low confidence level might be far too optimistic, given the widespread disagreement on fundamental moral questions. As ethics and political scholars can attest, there are still major debates over our basic moral duties to each other. The fact that experts disagree on controversial moral topics, such as criminal justice reform and abortion rights, suggests that we should be less confident about many of our moral beliefs. As such, the probability of avoiding moral catastrophe might be much lower than the 46 percent example. If this is true, then future generations will likely condemn many of the common beliefs and practices of our time as deeply immoral.

Due to the inductive and disjunctive worry arguments, Williams claims it is very likely that society is committing moral catastrophes right now, and that each of us is complicit in at least some of them. As in the past, our current moral beliefs are shaped and influenced by culture and upbringing, making moral catastrophes hard to recognize since they are widely accepted.

Williams claims that it is morally urgent to identify and stop current moral catastrophes. He proposes three ways to do this: (1) by studying ethics, (2) by studying the current state of the world through the sciences, and (3) by encouraging dialogue between philosophical ethics and the sciences, which are sometimes isolated in their "ivory towers." Once a moral catastrophe has been identified, the next important and difficult task is to implement changes to end it.

Within the effective altruist community, there is ongoing debate and disagreement over which current practices constitute moral catastrophes. Some possible examples identified by effective altruists include indifference to global extreme poverty, lack of investment in preventing future catastrophic events like pandemics, indifference to our impact on future lives, and the way we treat animals on a mass scale, which we will explore next. With this framework of moral catastrophes in mind, let's now move to a specific case that effective altruists often argue is a moral catastrophe: factory farming.

3.2 Is factory farming a moral catastrophe?

The traditional image of farm animals living their lives on spacious fields represents only a tiny fraction of what actually happens. Researchers from a 2019 study concluded that 99 percent of farmed animals in the United States and more than 90 percent of the world's farmed animals live within factory farms.[4] Factory farms, also sometimes called concentrated animal feeding operations, keep animals in high-stock densities to minimize costs. In severely crowded spaces, animals often lack room to move freely or even turn around. They sometimes suffocate or attack each other due to the stresses of confinement. We will not go into the disturbing details of the often miserable lives of these animals, but, in short, factory farms prioritize production and profit over the wellbeing of animals. If nonhuman animals have at least some moral value, and we have some degree of ethical duty to not abuse them or subject them to unnecessary suffering, factory farming is an immense moral problem and one that is growing larger over time.

Each year, more than 80 billion farm animals are slaughtered for meat production (not including seafood).[5] Figure 3.1 provides a visual representation to help put the scale of animals killed into perspective. The number of farm animals killed for meat is ten times the total human population (8 billion) and more than one thousand times the number of human deaths each year (around 60 million). Meat consumption tends to increase as countries become wealthier.[6] As a result, emerging economies such as China are driving up the demand for meat, which has led to a rapid rise in the number of animals raised and slaughtered in factory farms. If we accept that animals warrant moral consideration, then the enormous and growing scale of factory farming poses a moral crisis.

Whether factory farming is a moral catastrophe depends on assumptions about the moral status of animals. Do animals deserve moral consideration? There are two main views on this question: anthropocentrism and sentiocentrism. Anthropocentrism holds that we owe moral consideration to animals insofar as they benefit humans. In this view, animals

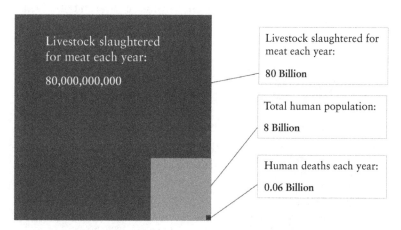

Figure 3.1: Livestock slaughtered for meat each year
Source: Author's figure based on data from Hannah Ritchie, Pablo Rosado, and Max Roser, "Meat and Dairy Production," *Our World in Data* (December 2023).

have only instrumental value, meaning they are valuable only because of their usefulness to humans, not for their own sake. Given this, animals are mere resources meant to serve humanity. However, this does not mean that anthropocentrists think we can treat animals however we want. Some argue for legal restrictions on animal abuse for two reasons. First, animal suffering can cause human distress; limiting cruelty can reduce human psychological harm. Second, people who abuse animals might be more likely to abuse other humans. Requiring some level of humane animal treatment can promote an overall virtue of kindness, improving our treatment of humans.

Nonetheless, anthropocentrists do not see factory farming and meat production as inherently immoral. They only object when farming practices harm humans in some tangible way, such as by upsetting them emotionally. Keeping farm animal suffering hidden can minimize that harm. Some anthropocentrists even deny that animals can suffer, claiming they are not capable of conscious experience. Others admit that animals may have the capacity to suffer but only give moral weight to human suffering.

On the other hand, sentiocentrism is the view that nonhuman animals can have intrinsic value – meaning they are valuable for their own sake, not just for humans.[7] Sentiocentrism rejects the idea that humans are the only animals that deserve moral consideration. Instead of

> **Instrumental value**: Something that is valuable because of what it produces or leads to. It derives its worth from its consequences.
> **Intrinsic value**: Something that is valuable for its own sake, not because of what it leads to. It has worth in and of itself.
> *Test for intrinsic value*: Ask "Why do you value this thing?" then "Would you still value it even if it didn't lead to those other results?" If yes, then it has intrinsic value.
> **Anthropocentrists** see animals as only having instrumental value – they matter based on their usefulness to humans.
> **Sentiocentrists** claim animals have intrinsic value as conscious, feeling beings – they matter for their own sake, not just what they can provide us.

focusing on what species you belong to, sentiocentrists claim that sentience – the ability to have subjective experiences – is what makes an individual morally valuable. Sentiocentrists believe we should respect the interests of animals for their own sake, as fellow beings who can feel and perceive.

Ignoring animal interests merely because they belong to a different species is what ethicists call speciesism. Philosophers like Peter Singer and Tom Regan argue that species membership alone is not a morally relevant criterion. They compare speciesism to racism and sexism – discriminating against others based on arbitrary characteristics of individuals. To illustrate this, imagine your favorite nonhuman science fiction or fantasy character; would it be morally acceptable to enslave, torture, or eat characters such as Chewbacca, simply because they are not human? The obvious answer, for most people, is no. To say otherwise is to be speciesist. Speciesism involves favoring the interests of one species, usually your own species, and disregarding the interests of other species for no reason other than species membership.

Avoiding speciesism does not mean treating all species the exact same way. Just as we consider different interests, abilities, and needs in our treatment of other humans, sentiocentrists claim that we should do the same for animals. For example, pigs do not care about voting but share interests in things like avoiding pain and enjoying space to move around and explore. Singer calls this idea the principle of equal consideration: we should give equal consideration to the interests of other sentient beings, regardless of their external characteristics; all sentient beings deserve moral concern for their interests.[8]

For sentiocentrists, our current treatment of animals is a moral catastrophe. They generally agree that speciesism is widespread in our culture, enabling the exploitation of animals for food, research, and entertainment. However, sentiocentrists disagree on both the severity of the moral catastrophe and how to solve it. For example, significant disagreement comes from two broad camps of sentiocentrists, those who promote animal welfare and those who emphasize animal rights.

Some sentiocentrists, such as Peter Singer, are proponents of animal welfare. Animal welfarists focus on the quality of life of animals and call for their better treatment. Singer claims that even a modest respect for the wellbeing of farm animals would require radical changes in our farming methods and our diets.[9]

Other sentiocentrists, such as Tom Regan, focus on animal rights. Regan claimed that any use of animals is immoral exploitation; since animals are conscious beings, they have inherent value and, as such, have the right to be treated as subjects, never used as mere objects. Proponents of animal rights tend to take a more hardline stance, such as advocating for the total abolishment of the use of animals in science and agriculture.[10]

While both animal welfare and animal rights approaches agree that our current treatment of farm animals is a moral catastrophe, animal rights proponents are more likely to consider it as an extremely urgent and severe catastrophe that demands the complete abolition of animal use, not just incremental welfare reforms.

In summary, there is a broad range of views regarding the moral status of animals, from completely disregarding their interests to advocating the total abolition of all animal use. Between these extremes, uncertainty lingers around the appropriate level of moral consideration to give to animals. The debate between animal welfare and animal rights perspectives underscores the moral uncertainty concerning our moral duties to animals – even among those who agree that current practices are wrong. The next section explores methods for navigating through such moral uncertainties.

3.3 Moral uncertainty: Veganism and moral caution

How much moral consideration should we give to animals? How confident should we be of our views on this issue? A common view among effective altruists is that we should admit our moral uncertainties on hard ethical questions and factor those uncertainties into our decision-making. People are used to managing uncertainty in everyday situations, such as planning their weekends based on the chance of rain. If we routinely manage uncertainty in our daily lives, perhaps we should also consider the implications of our moral uncertainties and factor them into our ethical reasoning.

The book *Moral Uncertainty*, by William MacAskill, Krister Bykvist, and Toby Ord, gives three main reasons why we should be morally uncertain.[11] The first is moral disagreement. As we saw in the previous section, there are many different views on how we should treat animals. Many moral views that were widely accepted in the past are now seen as morally repugnant. On this issue and many other moral issues, intelligent people disagree, including experts and researchers.

The second reason for moral uncertainty is the difficulty of ethics. Ethics requires tackling hard questions and weighing many different arguments on a given topic. It is a challenging field to study, made worse by the fact that people often have preconceived biases on moral issues.

A third reason for moral uncertainty is overconfidence: people tend to be too confident in their beliefs overall. In psychology, this is known as the overconfidence effect: people tend to be more confident in their beliefs than they should be based on the information given to them. In fact, research suggests that when people say they are 100 percent sure about something, they are wrong about 20 percent of the time. Studies on this topic are based on beliefs about claims that can be checked and verified, such as the correct spelling of a word.[12] However, for moral claims, about what is right or wrong, there is no agreed-upon way to test or verify them. This suggests that we should be even more uncertain about our moral beliefs compared to verifiable claims, such as how to spell difficult words.

How should we decide what to do when we are morally uncertain? There are two main approaches: my favorite theory

> **Moral uncertainty:** Uncertainty about how to act given a lack of certainty concerning moral principles, theories, and/or beliefs.
> **My favorite theory (MFT) approach:** Act as if the moral beliefs you are most confident in are correct, even if you are not certain.
> **Maximize expected choice-worthiness (MEC) approach:** Consider both the probabilities of different moral beliefs are correct and the magnitude of their choice-worthiness (how bad or good would the action be if the moral belief were correct).

(MFT) and maximize expected choice-worthiness (MEC).[13] The MFT approach says that we should act according to the moral principles, theories, and beliefs that we think are most likely to be true. This is how most people naturally tend to make moral decisions. MFT tells us to act as if the moral beliefs we are most sure of are true, even if we cannot be certain that they are.

The second approach is to maximize expected choice-worthiness. MEC tells us that we should consider both the probabilities of different moral beliefs being true and the magnitude of their choice-worthiness (how significant would they be if true). MEC says that we should take our uncertainty into account, especially in cases that could result in severe moral wrongdoing.

One possible outcome of using MEC is moral caution – if there is a reasonable chance that an action is extremely wrong, we should avoid doing it, because of the moral risk. For example, imagine driving on a highway on a cold winter night and seeing something that might be a small child walking on the side of the road. You think it is probably not a child, but there is a reasonable chance that it is. If what you saw was a child, it would be very wrong to leave a child in such danger. On the other hand, if there is no child, you would only lose a minute or two by turning around and checking. Moral caution says that it is better to turn around and check, just in case.

Moral caution is the principle of taking morally risky actions seriously, given the potentially severe wrongdoing they may involve, even if you think other assessments of the action are more likely to be true.[14] Of course, for a moral view to be worth considering, you need to view that perspective as having a reasonable chance of being true, even if improbable.

Let's explore another example: veganism – the practice of refraining from consuming animal products. According to the MFT approach, whether you should be vegan depends on what moral view you think is most convincing. If you think it is more likely than not that eating animals is morally permissible, then MFT says that you should assume there is nothing wrong with consuming them. If you agree with the animal welfare or rights views and think it is more probable that consuming animal products is wrong, then you should not consume them. You should think carefully about what moral theory or principles on this topic are most reasonable to you, but once you weigh the different arguments, you should act according to the moral view that you are most confident in.

On the other hand, the MEC approach takes into account both how probable you think each moral view is and how significant the action would be if that view were true. If anthropocentric views are correct, there is nothing wrong with consuming animal products, but also nothing wrong with avoiding them. Both vegan and nonvegan diets are morally permissible. If the animal rights or welfare views are correct, consuming animal products would be severely wrong, taking part in a system that causes immense suffering for billions of animals each year. If you find sentiocentrist views as at least reasonably possible, consuming animal products is morally risky. In this case, using the MEC approach would suggest moral caution and avoiding animal products. A nonvegan diet risks major wrongdoing without a comparable moral upside. MEC seems to suggest that, in the case of veganism, we should treat animals as if they have moral value, even if we are not completely sure whether they do or not, because of how terrible it would be if they are conscious beings that suffer greatly because of our actions.

The MEC approach is common among effective altruists; however, William MacAskill cautions about oversimplifying its application. Moral deliberations involve many intersecting beliefs. When considering moral uncertainty at each intersection, applying MEC becomes complicated. For veganism, there are uncertainties about the level of suffering that animals experience, whether some animals can live happy lives on farms, how much animals matter morally, and the personal and financial costs of adopting a countercultural diet. Taking moral uncertainty seriously, as the MEC approach recommends, is not an easy task. Nonetheless, MacAskill is a proponent of the approach. He agrees that MEC usually involves avoiding morally risky actions given reasonably possible views, while, at the same time, attempting to maximize the good you can do given the constraints of moral caution.[15]

The MEC approach is a variation of expected value theory, which is arguably the core strategy used by effective altruists in dealing with uncertainty. Even with consideration for moral caution, uncertainty remains about whether avoiding animal products actually reduces animal suffering. The next section explores expected value theory as another way to handle uncertainty.

3.4 Expected value: Does your diet make a difference?

Expected value (EV) is the practice of estimating the value of actions with uncertain outcomes. EV is often used in economics, investing, insurance, and game theory to assess the risks and benefits of different choices under uncertainty. In statistics, the basic definition of EV is the amount that we can expect to gain or lose from an action multiplied by the likelihood of that gain or loss. A simple formula for this, when there are only two possible outcomes, is the following:

EV = (gain × probability of gain) − (loss × probability of loss)

EV is the amount of gain multiplied by the chance of that gain, minus the amount of loss multiplied by the chance of that loss.

A good way to explain expected value is by using gambling examples, where we can measure the probabilities and outcomes clearly. For example, imagine a friend offering you a wager based on flipping a coin. If the coin lands on heads, she will give you $5. If it lands on tails, you will give her $10. Without using a formula, you might be able to tell that this is a bad bet for you. However, we can do a formal calculation to illustrate this. The EV of this wager for you is −$2.50 [($5 × 0.5) − ($10 × 0.5) = −$2.5].

But what does this number mean? In no outcome are you losing $2.50; you are either gaining $5 or losing $10. Essentially, what this number means is that if you make this same bet a lot of times, you will lose on average $2.50 per bet. So, if you made this bet 1,000 times, you can expect to lose around $2,500. In fact, the more games that are played, the closer the average returns will be to the calculated EV. This mathematical principle is called the law of large numbers (also known as the law of averages).[16]

The law of large numbers is how casinos can offer big jackpots and still make huge profits. Almost all bets at casinos are bad bets for the gamblers, with negative EV, in terms of money.[17] For example, in the game of American roulette, for each $1 you bet on a single number, if the ball lands on that number, you will win $35. If it does not, you lose your bet. The roulette wheel gives an illusion of fair odds by having thirty-six black and red numbers (#1–36). However, there are an additional two green numbers (0 and 00), which gives the casino a house edge. As a result, the EV for those making this bet is around −5.3% [(35 × 1/38) − (1 × 37/38)]. This means that, on average, you will lose about 5 cents for every dollar you bet on this game.

Some roulette players will win huge payouts from the casino. But this is more than offset by the losses that gamblers incur over the course of the many games played at the table. This is why the house always wins. The EV of each bet is positive for the casino and negative for the players. As long as many bets are made, the casino will make more money than it loses on average per bet. The more bets made, the better for the casino.

Gamblers are typically aware that casino games have a house edge, or, in other words, that bets at casinos have a negative EV. If that is the case, why do people gamble? For some, a weekend of casino gambling with the expectation of losing money may still have an overall positive EV. This is because we value more than just money. We exchange a loss of money for other things we value on a daily basis, whether that is an experience, such as going to a movie with friends, or tangible objects, like new clothes. For some people who enjoy playing casino games, the expected loss of money comes with the expected gain of enjoyable experiences.

However, it should be noted that for some people with addictive tendencies, casino gaming may come with far more risks than simply monetary loss. Millions of Americans suffer from gambling addiction disorders, resulting in damaged relationships and immense psychological distress.[18] So, for some people, gambling comes with the EV of an enjoyable weekend, win or lose; for others, gambling comes with significant risks to their financial stability and mental health.

One area of uncertainty that expected value can help address is whether being vegan actually reduces the number of animals killed each year. One objection to veganism is that a single person boycotting animal products might not meaningfully decrease the actual number of animals harmed. So, you could be making a personal sacrifice without changing anything. By refusing to buy animal products, an individual does not directly help the animals already killed and stocked on the store shelves. However, it is an open question whether a person's boycott reduces the overall production of animal products.

This is an important issue not just for vegans, but for any consumer movement aiming to impact production through reduced purchasing of goods. In a world of mass production, how much does one person abstaining from a product affect the output of those goods? It seems possible that each individual's impact is very small. Yet it seems clear that if millions change their habits, production will fall from the decreased demand. Suppliers will not continue to order more of a product if it does not sell. We don't know how often suppliers reduce orders based on demand, which eventually affects production, but we know it happens some of the time. So, when one person avoids animal products, it is uncertain if each individual choice will reduce production. However, we can assume that sometimes those choices do so.

Expected value can help address the uncertainty over whether one person reducing consumption of animal products makes a difference. Using EV principles, we can estimate the impact of veganism. As with gambling, you may not know what the outcomes will be, but you can calculate the EV if you know the probabilities of the results. Given the complexities of modern food production, this is challenging to assess as individuals. However, economists have applied EV principles to estimate how much production falls on average when a person abstains from purchasing animal-based goods.

Economists Bailey Norwood and Jayson Lusk estimate that, on average, giving up ten pounds of animal products results in a fall in production by five to nine pounds over time. For example, when a person reduces their milk consumption by one gallon per month, over time, milk production falls by around half a gallon per month. Although not a 1:1 ratio, when demand falls for a product, production of that product tends to fall as well. Norwood and Lusk estimate that, depending on the animal product given up, due to market dynamics, production falls by different rates, as summarized in Table 3.1.[19] While vegans cannot be certain of the exact impact of their dietary choices, these estimates suggest that they can expect their actions to reduce the overall production of animal-based products over time compared to a typical diet. This means, on average, fewer animals are raised and killed in factory farms.

One important consideration concerns the number of animal deaths that result from plant-based food production.

Table 3.1: Reduction of animal products by weight

Giving up 1 lb of animal products	Eventual reduced production
Eggs	0.91 lb
Chicken	0.76 lb
Pork	0.74 lb
Beef	0.68 lb
Milk	0.56 lb

Source: Author's table adapted from F. Bailey Norwood and Jayson L. Lusk, *Compassion, by the Pound* (2011).

Creating plant-based food also results in animal deaths through farming practices, such as habitat destruction and pest control. However, most farmed animals are fed more pounds of crops than the weight of meat produced. For example, one acre of corn provides enough calories for an individual for one year; however, to produce the equivalent number of calories from chicken, it takes almost five acres of corn for livestock feed.[20] As such, replacing animal-based food with plant-based food still reduces overall animal lives lost due to agriculture.

Even if you accept that reducing animal product consumption likely leads to fewer animal products produced in factory farms, the extent to which you should prioritize reducing animal consumption still depends on a variety of value judgments. Effective altruists sometimes refer to this as assigning moral weights. In terms of animal consumption, important moral weights to consider are the moral significance of unnecessary animal killing compared to unnecessary animal suffering. If you prioritize reducing the number of farm animals killed, then focusing on a diet that reduces the consumption of smaller animals may have the best expected value. For example, reducing chicken consumption results in fewer chickens being produced and killed compared to reducing beef consumption, given that cows are significantly larger animals.

Some individuals opt to reduce their beef intake, often for environmental or health reasons, and replace it with poultry. However, this dietary choice would likely result in more individual animals being slaughtered over time. To provide context, Americans consume more than 270 pounds of meat annually.[21] This is equivalent to the meat produced from approximately fifty-four chickens or only half a cow.[22] On the other hand, if your goal is to reduce overall suffering in factory farms, it makes sense to account for the intensity of suffering for each type of animal due to common farming practices. In this case, it might be more effective to focus on reducing pork consumption, since pigs have high cognitive abilities but often suffer terrible conditions on farms.[23]

However, the number of animals it takes to produce a serving of meat is relevant here, too. Since it requires killing more smaller animals to produce the same amount of food as killing a single larger animal, eating smaller animals can lead to more total days lived in suffering for farm animals overall. If you aim to reduce the total number of days lived in suffering by animals, reducing fish and chicken consumption might be best. For instance, researchers estimate that six days of animal suffering goes into producing every serving of breaded chicken and sixteen days of suffering for every serving of battered fish fillet; whereas only half a day of suffering goes into each serving of breaded pork chops.[24] However, you might give more moral weight to that half a day of suffering of a pig given its higher cognitive abilities. If you weigh each day of suffering for a pig as over thirty times more morally significant than a day of suffering for a fish or over twelve times that of a chicken, it might make sense to favor eating them instead.

As we have seen, anthropocentrists believe animals have no intrinsic value and as such, would assign no moral weight to their lives and suffering. In this case, reducing animal suffering has no moral value. However, even if we care about animals only in relation to how they affect humans, reducing the consumption of animal products may still have a positive expected value if it reduces the environmental impact of our diet. Animal-based foods typically have far greater carbon footprints than plant-based foods. For example, for each pound of food produced, beef generates around 93 pounds of greenhouse gas emissions, whereas tofu produces only around 3 pounds.[25]

Despite the complexities surrounding veganism and the impacts of dietary choices, most effective altruists try to reduce their consumption of animal products.[26] Many of them view reducing animal product consumption as the safest option due to considerations of both moral caution and expected value.

Box 3.1: Expected value (EV) in practice: Does a pescatarian diet do more harm than good?

Garrison Lovely, journalist and effective altruist, decided to reduce his meat intake for ethical reasons by switching to a pescatarian diet, which excludes all meat except seafood. He estimated this would improve his diet's EV by reducing harm in two ways:

1. Fish have a much smaller carbon footprint than other animal proteins.
2. He viewed fish as less likely to be worthy of compassion compared to land animals.

Pescatarianism is often seen as a more ethical option for meat-eaters looking to reduce harm from their diet but not ready to go fully vegetarian or vegan. However, Lovely later reassessed his decision through the lens of EV of his dietary change. He concluded that although he may have decreased his carbon footprint, his pescatarian diet likely did more harm than good overall for three main reasons:

1. Recent studies suggest fish may feel pain, have emotions, and complex social relationships, although

expressed differently from land animals. Lovely no longer deemed fish less likely to be sentient.
2. Production of fish may involve more suffering than land animals. Increasingly, fish are also factory-farmed in densely packed, disease-prone conditions. Wild-caught fish often experience excruciating deaths from suffocation, being cut open alive, or being crushed in nets. Fish get little legal protection from cruelty laws compared to land animals.
3. It takes far more fish lives to replace the same amount of protein as land animals. For example, a farmed salmon is fed more than 100 fish in its lifetime. Per salmon produced, more than 1,000 fish are killed. As for wild-caught fish, the practice inevitably involves bycatch – which results in the unintended deaths of other marine animals, such as turtles, sharks, and marine mammals.

Humans catch or farm staggering numbers of fish globally each year, an estimated 850 billion to 2.5 trillion, dwarfing the number of land farm animals killed. This enormous scale magnifies the harm resulting from fish consumption.

Although well-intentioned, Garrison Lovely now views his year as a pescatarian as having done more harm than good compared to his previous diet when analyzed through an EV framework. As a result, he has adopted a fully vegetarian diet.

Source: Based on Garrison Lovely, "Pescatarians are Responsible for Many More Animal Deaths than Regular Meat Eaters," *Vox*, March 16, 2023, https://www.vox.com/future-perfect/23639475/pescetarian-eating-fish-ethics-vegetarian-animal-welfare-seafood-fishing-chicken-beef-climate.

3.5 Problems with expected value

Although expected value is a standard tool used in many domains, such as business, insurance, and gambling, it is not without its problems and limitations. This section will briefly explore a few of these issues and how effective altruists respond to them.

One potential problem is that it could lead to prioritizing options that have high-value outcomes even when they are extremely unlikely to occur.[27] This might overemphasize long-shot options that are extremely unlikely to yield any results. Many people are uncomfortable with high-risk, high-reward strategies, even if they have the highest calculated EV. However, some effective altruists see this as an advantage, not a disadvantage, of expected value theory. They believe EV can help identify overlooked issues and options dismissed due to low probability that deserve more consideration given the significance of their potential outcomes.

Based on this, some effective altruists advocate for a "hits-based" approach to giving and to doing good. The hits-based approach to giving involves focusing on maximizing the expected value in your donations by supporting projects that have a high risk of failure but a huge impact if they succeed.[28] This means that you should expect most of your donations to do little to nothing; however, this is offset by the "hits," the few projects you support that are immensely successful. The hope is that the successes have such a significant impact that you end up doing far more good overall with your limited resources. This is similar to a common venture capitalist strategy called moonshot investing: investing in numerous high-risk, high-reward ventures in the hope that the large returns of the successes make up for the losses.

Effective altruists also take other approaches to this issue, such as the diversified portfolio approach and the data-driven safe-bets approach. The diversified portfolio approach is similar to common financial investment strategies that reduce risk by diversifying investments. Applying this to philanthropic giving, the aim is to allocate donations to some low-risk, high-evidence strategies that have a high probability of success, and some high-risk, high-reward strategies that have a high probability of failure but a huge potential impact if successful. Others opt for the data-driven safe-bets approach, focusing on the most evidence-backed, low-risk options so that they can be confident that their donations are doing good.[29] However, this might overemphasize charities whose outcomes are easier to measure. This leads us to the next problem: quantification.

For many important decisions, such as how to reduce animal suffering, probabilities and outcomes are difficult to estimate confidently. EV works best when there are clear probabilities of outcomes and values for those outcomes. A key difference between applying EV to gambling problems compared to world ethical problems is that we lack reliable data for probabilities and outcomes that can be used in formal EV calculations. When we are uncertain about the inputs, we also should be uncertain about the EV outputs.

In response to this problem, effective altruists often point out that rough calculations can still be useful, as shown by the use of Fermi estimates in the sciences. Fermi estimates, also known as back-of-the-envelope calculations, involve making rough estimates of things that are hard or impossible to measure accurately by breaking a problem down into smaller, simpler parts. Having some estimate is better than having no estimate when dealing with uncertainty. Rough, ballpark estimates can assist with decision-making when dealing with difficult problems. Nonetheless, there is still uncertainty about how much confidence and weight we should give to these estimates.

This leads us to a meta-problem for expected value: uncertainty about how to deal with uncertainty itself. This problem concerns the inherent uncertainty of how much confidence we should give to using expected value in our decision-making. This can lead to a regressive problem where we are not only uncertain about various moral beliefs and values in the world, but we also have to be uncertain about which approach to uncertainty is the right one.

Effective altruists have different views on how much we should rely on expected value in decision-making. Some argue that although EV is a flawed tool, it is the best one available and should guide all decision-making, including moral choices. Others believe we should use EV as one of many tools to improve decision-making. They see it as a useful tool, but not one to be exclusively relied upon; one among many tools.

Effective altruist organizations generally agree with the latter view: EV is a helpful tool that can guide decisions on doing good under uncertainty, although not the only tool.[30] They generally value it but also recognize the problems explored in this chapter, such as the challenges of accurate quantification and moral weights. As such, effective altruist organizations often highlight expected value as an important but not sole consideration in overall decision-making.

3.6 How effective altruists combat factory farming

This chapter has focused on how our individual lifestyle choices can reduce harm, given various uncertainties. Reducing consumption of animal products or going completely vegan are ways in which individuals can potentially decrease the negative impacts associated with their diets. However, many effective altruist organizations recommend additional actions beyond individual diet changes to more significantly impact the issue of factory farming,[31] including the following:

- *Advocacy for improved animal policies.* Supporting and engaging in social advocacy can lead to policy changes by governments and industries that can create better conditions for farmed animals. For example, in 2018, California voters passed Proposition 12, a ballot measure that set regulations

for more space for confined animals and banned sales of animal products from noncompliant out-of-state producers. Influencing broader changes through advocacy takes many forms, from grassroots campaigns and movement building to outreach and education.
- *Supporting plant-based meat alternatives.* Plant-based meat alternatives could reduce demand for factory-farmed meat. Companies like Beyond Meat and Impossible Foods aim to create plant-based alternatives indistinguishable in taste from animal-based meat. The goal is to produce products that taste the same or better but are plant-based rather than sourced from animals. If such alternatives become cheaper and taste comparable, they could lessen demand for factory-farmed meat, reducing their production and the associated animal suffering.
- *Supporting high-impact animal charities.* Animal Charity Evaluators is an effective altruist organization that assesses animal nonprofits and recommends those with the highest expected impact from donations. In 2022, they recommended three groups as top charities working specifically to combat factory farming: (1) Faunalytics, which provides animal advocates with research to increase their effectiveness; (2) The Humane League, which uses tactics from grassroots campaigns to corporate outreach to help reduce animal suffering; and (3) The Good Food Institute, which researches and promotes alternatives to animal proteins. They also recommended Wild Animal Initiative, which focuses on research and advocacy to improve the welfare of wild animals (rather than farm animals).

Both individual and collective action are important to drive progress on moral issues. While individual lifestyle choices matter, large global issues like factory farming often require systemic change. The next chapter will explore the topic of systemic change and how individuals can contribute to it in the context of addressing climate change.

Questions for reflection

1. What common current practices do you think are moral catastrophes that future generations will condemn us for? What should we do about them? Do you think factory farming is a moral catastrophe? Why or why not?
2. How much, if at all, do animals morally matter? Do some animals matter more than others? If so, why? Is your viewpoint closer to anthropocentrism or sentiocentrism? Explain your reasons.
3. What topics do you feel especially morally uncertain about? How do you think people should act, given moral uncertainty?
4. Give an example of applying expected value theory to a moral issue. What do you think are the strengths and weaknesses of this approach?

Classroom exercise

In small groups, first explore the Faunalytics graphs, "The Impact of Replacing Animal Products," https://faunalytics.org/animal-product-impact-scales/. Next, discuss what diet you think would have the highest expected value in terms of days of animal suffering, number of animals killed, and climate impact. What do you think is the most ethical diet, all things considered, and why? Share your group's conclusions. Finally, each group should share what uncertainties came up in your discussion. How did you deal with these uncertainties?

Helpful resources

Factory farming and animal welfare

Roman Duda, "Factory Farming: Why Helping to End Factory Farming Could Be the Most Important Thing You Could Do," *80,000 Hours*, February 2022. https://80000hours.org/problem-profiles/factory-farming/.

"Animal Welfare," *Probably Good*. https://probablygood.org/cause-areas/animal-welfare/.

Peter Singer, *Animal Liberation Now*. New York: Harper Perennial, 2023.

Speciesism, sentiocentrism, and intrinsic value

"Speciesism," *Animal Ethics*. https://www.animal-ethics.org/speciesism/.

"Definitions," *Sentience Research*. This page provides definitions of key terms related to animal sentience. This organization also provides collections of research concerning sentience in animals. https://sentience-research.org/definitions/.

"The Intrinsic Values Test," *Clearer Thinking*. This interactive tool helps people identify what they hold as intrinsically valuable. https://www.clearerthinking.org/tools/the-intrinsic-values-test.

Moral uncertainty

Benjamin Todd, "Moral Uncertainty: How to Act When You're Uncertain about What's Good," *80,000 Hours*, September 2021. https://80000hours.org/articles/moral-uncertainty/.

"We Probably Believe Morally Monstrous Things. What

Should We Do about That?" *The 80,000 Hours Podcast*, January 19, 2018. William MacAskill, interviewed by Robert Wiblin, produced by Keiran Harris. https://80000hours.org/podcast/episodes/will-macaskill-moral-philosophy/.

Expected value

Holden Karnofsky, "Expected Value," *Cold Takes*, December 17, 2021. https://www.cold-takes.com/expected-value/.

Benjamin Todd, "Expected Value: How Can We Make a Difference When We're Uncertain What's True?" *80,000 Hours*, April 2023. https://80000hours.org/articles/expected-value/.

Adam Steinberg, "Using Expected Value When Donating to Charity – and Day-to-Day," *Giving What We Can*, August 15, 2022. https://www.givingwhatwecan.org/blog/using-expected-value-when-donating-to-charity-and-day-to-day.

4

Systemic Change and Moral Pitfalls: Combating Climate Change

A common criticism of effective altruism is that it focuses too much on individual action and small-scale interventions rather than on the large systemic changes needed to solve our world's problems. However, in practice, effective altruists often advocate for systemic change. To do this effectively, we have to look for the ways that have the most significant impact on the policies and technologies that shape our society.

Combating climate change is a cause area that highlights effective altruists advocating for systemic change. Many effective altruist organizations, such as 80,000 Hours, list climate change among the world's most pressing problems.[1] In this chapter, we will explore effective altruist approaches to combating climate change and how effective altruist organizations, such as Giving Green and Founders Pledge, advocate for individuals to contribute to systemic solutions. We'll also examine the potential of lifestyle changes and the dangers of moral licensing.

What can we do to combat climate change most effectively? Although there is no single solution, we will explore throughout this chapter many strategies that effective altruists propose. As we will see, there are numerous ways we can make a difference. However, there are also many altruistic pitfalls, ways that we might think are helping but that make the problem worse in practice. We'll first explore one potential pitfall: carbon offsets, a proposed solution to climate change that, in many cases, may do more harm than good.

4.1 Carbon offsets controversy

A common approach to combating climate change is to purchase carbon offsets, which aim to compensate for the greenhouse gas emissions that you or your organization produce. Greenhouse gases (GHG) make the earth warmer by trapping more heat in the atmosphere over time, a process known as the greenhouse effect. Increased levels of GHG emissions by humanity since the Industrial Revolution are the root cause of our current climate crisis. By supporting projects that reduce GHG emissions or remove them from the atmosphere, carbon offsets aim to balance out the emissions we are responsible for. However, carbon offsets are controversial because they may not deliver the climate benefits they claim and may even create perverse incentives that increase GHG emissions overall.

To see how this could be the case, let's review some relevant background information. GHG emissions are quantified in terms of carbon dioxide-equivalents (CO_2e). CO_2e is a measure that expresses the global warming potentials of different GHGs using the warming effect of CO_2 as a baseline. Understanding the range of greenhouse gases and their varying warming potentials is necessary for accurate assessments of carbon offset projects. Carbon dioxide (CO_2) is the most abundant GHG, but others, like methane and nitrous oxide, trap much more heat per ton emitted. For example, methane has 28 times the warming effect of the same amount of CO_2, nitrous oxide has 265 times the warming effect, and some industrial gases, such as fluorocarbons (f-gases), generate thousands of times more warming per ton emitted.[2]

Given the urgency and scale of climate change, many environmentally conscious individuals, organizations, and businesses turn to carbon offset programs to mitigate their

Systemic Change and Moral Pitfalls

GHG emissions. Carbon offsets, in theory, allow individuals and organizations to reduce their overall climate impact by supporting projects that prevent or reduce GHG emissions or remove them from the atmosphere. The average person in the United States emits around 18 tons of CO_2e annually,[3] far above the sustainable global target of less than 2 tons. The concept is straightforward: if your lifestyle generates 18 tons of CO_2e, you could pay organizations to offset those emissions by reducing or sequestering an equivalent amount. In doing so, you could theoretically become net-neutral, or even net-negative, regarding your overall carbon footprint.

However, researchers have questioned whether carbon offset programs deliver meaningful climate benefits. Independent researchers claim that most carbon offset providers overstate the actual emission reductions of their programs, and many so-called carbon offsets may not have any benefit at all. In many cases, the programs sound good in theory, but the mechanisms they are based on do not make a difference in practice. Three primary reasons for this are leakage, non-additionality, and non-permanence. Let's go over each of these.

1. *Leakage*: Some projects shift emissions from one area to another instead of reducing them. Plugging one hole in a bucket may only change the leak to another hole slightly above it. For example, protecting one section of forest may not reduce the number of trees cut down, as foresters can move their operations to cut down trees in other areas instead.
2. *Non-additionality*: Some projects would have happened anyway, with or without the additional money from selling carbon offsets. For example, a new wind farm may have been built without the extra money collected from selling carbon offsets. In this case, carbon offsets should be measured on the benefits of any additional wind turbines constructed due to the carbon offset sales, if any.
3. *Non-permanence*: Some projects sequester carbon only temporarily before it is later released, and so are not

permanent solutions. For example, planting trees helps capture carbon from the air, but only for as long as the trees live. Once they die, decompose, or are burned, that carbon is released back into the atmosphere through GHGs such as CO_2 and methane. As such, the lifespan of the trees and risks such as forest fires should be taken into account.

Even if the projects are well designed and implemented, many carbon offset programs exaggerate the amount of emissions they reduce or avoid. In 2023, Guardian and Corporate Accountability researchers investigated the top fifty carbon offset projects. They categorized 78 percent of them as probable junk or worthless, meaning they likely had no real climate benefit due to fundamental program flaws. They often use unrealistic assumptions or overly optimistic estimates to calculate the impact of the offsets they sell. Another 16 percent looked problematic and potentially worthless. The remaining 6 percent did not have enough available evidence for their claims to be independently verified. Astonishingly, the researchers estimated that more than $1 billion had already been spent on the carbon offsets that were likely junk or worthless.[4]

What about offsets that are independently certified? Carbon offset registries claim to vet projects before listing them on their websites for purchase. These third-party organizations certify their listed projects and issue certificates for purchased offsets for each ton of CO_2e reduced or avoided. Some of the leading registries are Verra (also called the Verified Carbon Standard), ACR (American Carbon Registry), and CAR (Climate Action Reserve). However, even certified offsets are not immune to criticism.

Researchers have found that the impact of certified offsets were also prone to exaggeration due to issues such as leakage, non-additionality, and non-permanence. For example, a 2022 analysis of one of the largest carbon offset certifiers, Verra, deemed over 90 percent of their certified rainforest carbon offsets to be worthless.[5] Another 2022 study of almost 300 certified forest carbon offsets found issues across top registries, concluding that standard protocols used by registries often result in substantial inflation of the value of the carbon offsets purchased from them.[6]

Overstating the cost-effectiveness of a carbon offset program can lead to phantom offsets – carbon offsets that someone has purchased but that did not reduce GHG emissions. Consequently, this can lead to a net increase in emissions by those who buy them. For example, imagine Bob, concerned about his carbon footprint, decides to purchase carbon offsets whenever he travels by airplane. Since he is now offsetting his flights, he no longer feels morally conflicted by air travel; as a result, he takes many more flights each year. He pays for carbon offsets for each flight, thinking they negate the impact on global warming. Unfortunately, if most of those carbon offsets are phantom offsets, as researchers suggest, Bob likely had a net increase in his carbon footprint, all while believing his travels were carbon neutral or even having a negative carbon footprint. As such, even if a carbon offset program reduces GHG emissions, by exaggerating the climate impact of its offset purchases, it could be doing more harm than good overall.

Not all carbon offsets are created equal. While alarming flaws are common, it doesn't mean all projects are worthless. As we'll explore next, through careful research, effective altruists have identified evidence-backed, high-quality carbon offset programs. Even so, we should be cautious about assuming that we can become carbon neutral through them alone.

4.2 Giving Green and rethinking offsets

Since not all carbon offset projects are reliable, how can you tell which ones are worth supporting? Giving Green is a nonprofit organization that applies the principles of effective altruism to climate philanthropy in order to help donors make informed decisions.[7] In addition to evaluating other climate-giving opportunities, Giving Green assesses various carbon offset projects based on criteria such as costs, benefits, additionality, and permanence. Giving Green then recommends the highest-impact projects to donors who want to combat climate change. The carbon offset projects that Giving Green has assessed and recommends fall into two main categories: carbon removal and emission reduction.

Carbon removal is the process of taking carbon out of the atmosphere and storing it for as long as possible. Many projections of the earth's climate suggest that large-scale carbon removal is necessary by 2050 in order to limit warming to the international target of 2°C.[8] As of 2023, Giving Green recommends three carbon removal offset programs that use different carbon removal technologies:

1. *Climeworks* uses machines that capture CO_2 directly from the air and store it underground in Iceland, where it reacts with basalt rock and turns into stone. Climeworks sells offsets for around $1,200 per ton of CO_2 removed.
2. *Charm Industrial* converts biomass waste, such as corn stalks and wheat straw, into bio-oil and injects it deep underground, where it becomes part of the geological formation. This process uses plants to capture CO_2 from the atmosphere and then stores that carbon underground for thousands of years, a mechanism known as biomass carbon removal and storage. Charm Industrial sells offsets for around $600 per ton of CO_2 removed.
3. *MASH Makes* converts crop waste, which otherwise would be burned, into biochar. This biochar is then used as a beneficial soil amendment, storing the carbon in the ground for hundreds of years. MASH Makes sells offsets for around $160 per ton of CO_2 removed.[9]

Giving Green recommends all three programs as high-quality carbon removal offset options. However, they are expensive compared to other opportunities. Purchasing offsets equal to just one American's average annual GHG emissions would cost thousands of dollars. Some emission reduction programs have far better cost-effectiveness.

Rather than removing existing CO_2 from the atmosphere, emission reduction offset programs aim to prevent or reduce new emissions of CO_2 or other greenhouse gases. This can be achieved through switching to cleaner energy sources, improving efficiency, or changing production and consumption patterns. Giving Green recommends two emission reduction offset programs that use different approaches:

1. *BURN* manufactures and distributes fuel-efficient cookstoves in sub-Saharan Africa. These cookstoves use less fuel and produce far less smoke than the traditional ones they are replacing, reducing both GHG emissions and indoor air pollution. BURN sells offsets for around $30 per ton of CO_2 emissions prevented, but Giving Green's 2021 cost-effectiveness analysis suggests it might be even better than that, closer to $5 per ton.
2. *Tradewater* identifies, controls, and destroys old refrigerants and other gases with extreme warming potential, which are sometimes thousands of times more potent than CO_2. Tradewater prevents these GHG emissions from leaking into the atmosphere, and as a co-benefit, many of these emissions are also ozone-depleting substances. Tradewater sells offsets for around $18 per ton of CO_2e emissions prevented.[10]

Giving Green recommends both programs as high-quality carbon prevention offset options. In theory, an individual purchasing offsets from these programs equivalent to the average American's annual carbon emissions would only cost hundreds of dollars annually – far less than the carbon capture options. However, Giving Green notes that it is extremely difficult to reliably estimate how much GHG emissions are prevented or captured as a result of offsets purchased, even for the programs they recommend. As such, they recommend rethinking carbon offsets.

Giving Green suggests that a better way to think about carbon offsets is not as a direct way to achieve net-zero carbon emissions, but instead as an investment in green programs.[11] Some carbon offset programs are promising and benefit the climate, but their impact estimates are still unreliable. The carbon offset cost-effectiveness calculations are too uncertain to be able to tell whether you can become net-zero by purchasing them. By viewing offsets as an investment in the future, we can change our perspective on how we are making an impact with our green giving. Instead of looking for the cheapest offsets, we can look for the best investments that have the most potential to reduce GHGs in the atmosphere over time.

For example, Giving Green recommends that donors who want to support carbon removal should consider giving to portfolio funds that support and accelerate the development of carbon removal systems. These funds are called catalytic carbon removal portfolios, designed to catalyze further development of carbon removal programs and technology. Two funds that Giving Green recommends are Frontier and Milkywire. Frontier allows investors to buy carbon removal offsets in advance to give carbon removal programs the funds to fast-track the development and scaling of their projects. Milkywire manages the Climate Transformation Fund, which helps finance the research and development of carbon removal technology.[12] Carbon removal is currently expensive, and the programs are relatively small. The hope is that with enough investment, the cost of carbon removal will go down, and the scale of the programs will go up.

Overall, Giving Green advocates rethinking offsets to view them as investments in climate action instead of seeing them as a reliable means to achieve "net-zero" individual carbon footprints. Donors can support the development of innovative carbon removal and reduction solutions by giving to rigorous, vetted programs. However, while Giving Green provides recommendations for high-quality carbon offset projects, they prioritize donations to effective policy advocacy groups, which can have a far greater impact.

None of the organizations Giving Green recommends for carbon offsets make their top climate-giving recommendation list. Instead of carbon offset programs, the top organizations recommended by Giving Green are those that focus on larger systemic changes, which can have a much greater impact on combating global warming. Although carbon offsets can have a role in combating climate change, much bigger solutions are needed. As we will see next, many effective altruists agree that systemic change is essential to address climate change.

4.3 The need for systemic change

The carbon offset market will hopefully improve in the future. With more reliable assessment methods and increased availability of high-quality, well-vetted offset programs, individuals and businesses could theoretically offset their carbon footprint to become carbon neutral or even carbon negative. However, climate change is such a large global problem that becoming carbon neutral individually, while a good step, hardly makes a dent in solving the overall issue. To address such a large-scale global problem, more far-reaching solutions are needed. This is why Giving Green and other effective altruist organizations highlight the necessity of systemic change.

Implementing systemic solutions can drive widespread progress on climate change. Large-scale systems can influence the behavior of millions of individuals and improve standard practices across entire industries. Improving green technology is one important avenue for spurring system-wide change. Technological innovation can create solutions that are easily scaled and spread globally. Some examples are the innovations made in renewable energy. In just ten years, from 2009 to 2019, the cost of electricity from solar declined by almost 90 percent, and the cost of electricity from wind declined by

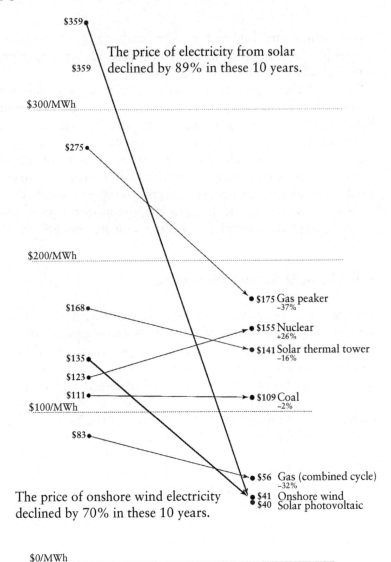

Figure 4.1: The price of electricity from new power plants
Source: Max Roser, "Why Did Renewables Become so Cheap so Fast?", *Our World in Data* (2023).

*Electricity prices are expressed in "levelized costs of energy" (LCOE). LCOE captures the cost of building the power plant itself as well as the ongoing costs for fuel and operating the power plant over its lifetime.

70 percent. This has made wind and solar the least expensive energy sources, cheaper than coal or gas.[13] Innovations in these technologies made them economically viable and scalable.

Due in part to their reduced costs, the US is steadily increasing the share of its renewable energy production. Since the 1960s, only around 5 percent of US energy came from renewables, but this began to sharply increase around 2009. In just over a decade, renewables have more than doubled to over 11 percent of US energy production today. Worldwide renewable energy followed similar trends, sharply increasing its share from around 7 percent to over 14 percent.[14]

In the United States, wind power generation now employs more people than coal production does. Amazingly, solar power employs more than five times as many people as coal production does and more than natural gas, oil, and coal energy generation combined.[15] The US still has progress to make, but solar and wind technological innovations are aiding the steady and rapid switch to renewable energy domestically and globally.

Another important avenue for enacting systemic change, which can work alongside green technological innovation, is improving governmental policies. Improving laws and regulations can reduce emissions across an entire industry within a country. Government policies help drive down costs and spur innovation in the renewable sector through subsidies and mandates. This helped scale the development and deployment of greener technologies, further reducing costs and enabling faster worldwide adoption. Some argue that the advances we have seen in green technology, such as wind and solar, would not have been possible without the help of government investment and regulation.[16]

For these reasons, effective altruist organizations like Giving Green highlight the importance of supporting and advocating for systemic change through both technological innovation and policy change. Together, they can help transition our energy systems to renewables and reduce greenhouse gas emissions globally.

In addition to Giving Green, another effective altruist organization that advocates for systemic change to combat climate change is Founders Pledge. This organization encourages entrepreneurs to commit to giving a portion of their proceeds to effective charities. To help guide its members toward impactful and informed giving, Founders Pledge conducts extensive research. One of the main cause areas they research is climate change philanthropy, where they analyze climate charities to offer guidance on the most effective giving strategies to combat global warming.

One organization that both Founders Pledge and Giving Green recommend is Clean Air Task Force, a nonprofit organization focused on addressing climate change through research and advocacy. Their work promotes clean energy solutions and policies through collaboration with governments and industries. In 2018, Founders Pledge conducted an extensive cost-effectiveness analysis of Clean Air Task Force. The report looked at the organization's past successes and at the resources needed to reach those achievements. Based on past successes, the estimated cost-effectiveness was an impressive $1.26 per ton of CO_2e emissions removed or prevented. Looking forward to future opportunities and building upon those past successes, the report estimated the cost-effectiveness of Clean Air Task Force in the future at an even more impressive $0.29 per ton of CO_2e emissions prevented or removed.[17] By influencing policy changes in governments and industries, systemic change can have a massive impact on reducing carbon emissions economy-wide.

Due to the enormous successes of these types of organizations, there have been major climate policy achievements in recent years. One prominent example is the US 2022 Climate Bill (the Inflation Reduction Act). This landmark bill allocated billions in funding toward combating climate change through supporting renewable energy, carbon capture, and a wide variety of other climate initiatives. However, it almost didn't happen, as there were several points during negotiations where it almost failed.[18] It succeeded in large part through the persistent effort and advocacy from climate action groups and the promotion of green policy through research from organizations like Clean Air Task Force. As a result of persistent effort, research, advocacy, and pressure, massive systemic change is possible.

Recognizing the need for systemic change in combating climate change, Giving Green and Founders Pledge's top donation recommendations focus on organizations that promote systemic change by improving governmental policies and investing in research and development of technological innovations that can be scaled globally. In addition to Clean Air Task Force, Founders Pledge also recommends donating to the organizations TerraPraxis and Carbon180.[19] Giving Green's 2023 top recommendations include Project InnerSpace, Opportunity Green, Industrious Labs, Good Food Institute, Good Energy Collective, and the Clean Air Task Force.[20] Giving Green estimates that their recommended high-impact nonprofits working on systemic change have a cost-effectiveness of around just \$1 per ton of CO_2e emissions prevented or removed.[21]

These recommendations are continually researched and updated as new evidence emerges on the highest-impact organizations combating climate change. As such, it can be difficult for individual donors and organizations to keep up with the latest developments in high-impact climate philanthropy. One option that can help with this is to give to expert-managed giving funds; in this way, donations are automatically directed to the highest-impact organizations, even as recommendations change over time. Both Giving Green and Founders Pledge manage climate change giving funds to which individuals and organizations can contribute.[22] As a result, donors don't have to update their giving each year based on new recommendations – these expert-managed funds do that work for them.

By supporting high-impact climate charities, individuals can help those organizations expand their services and better advocate for the broad systemic changes and policies needed to address global warming. However, for large, complex issues like climate change, there are no silver bullets and no single solutions. Many climate activists advocate for broad, multifaceted approaches, which may include donating to high-impact charities as one component. But many also advocate for individuals doing their part by adopting greener lifestyles. In the next section, we'll explore a general objection to focusing only on green giving and what individuals can do to live more sustainably.

4.4 What about lifestyle changes? Focus on the big stuff

Everyday lifestyles in affluent countries are often highly carbon-intensive compared to the rest of the world. Although individuals could, theoretically, offset those emissions by purchasing carbon offsets or donating to high-impact climate charities, many people concerned about climate change feel that this approach alone is not sufficient. It seems to lack integrity to be concerned about climate change while still engaging in some of the worst carbon-intensive practices, even if you contribute to climate charities or offsets. Some find it distasteful when climate philanthropists who donate substantial amounts to climate charities nonetheless engage in extremely carbon-intensive lifestyles. For instance, wealthy donors may frequently travel by private jet – one of the most carbon-intensive ways to travel. And even everyday individuals living in affluent countries often travel by gasoline-powered cars, which, as we will see, is also among the most carbon-intensive modes of travel.

Many climate activists argue that we need to take all actions available to us, big and small, to combat climate change. This includes acknowledging how our individual lifestyles are contributing to global warming and working on reducing our impact by developing greener habits. We'll go over some of the biggest ways you can reduce the carbon footprint of your lifestyle. However, as we'll see in the next section, there are dangers in overprioritizing individual lifestyle changes.

Nonetheless, they can still play a role in reducing our GHG emissions, especially if we focus on the biggest and easiest ways to live more sustainably. Although you likely can make a greater difference on climate change through careful donations to high-impact charities, living a greener lifestyle can help you become a better climate advocate and contribute to a culture of climate awareness and action.

The basic effective altruist approach focuses on the big stuff: look at your most significant emission sources, then identify how you can best reduce them. Home energy use, personal transportation, and food consumption are the three areas of a typical individual's lifestyle that have the largest climate impact. Together, they account for around 80 percent of an average individual's carbon footprint, with all other goods and services combined accounting for just 20 percent.[23] By focusing efforts on reducing the impact of these three major categories, individuals can drastically reduce their carbon footprint.

Food accounts for around 20 percent of an individual's carbon footprint in the United States.[24] What are the biggest ways to reduce the emissions from your diet? The main advice here is pretty straightforward, even if hard to implement for some: eat more plant-based foods and fewer animal products. According to a 2020 analysis by Hannah Ritchie, the most significant factor in your diet's carbon footprint is the type of food you eat. Some foods take far more greenhouse gas emissions to produce than others. For example, the production of a pound of beef emits around 60 pounds of greenhouse gases, while a pound of nuts only requires about 0.3 pounds – more than 200 times less. Animal-based foods tend to have far higher carbon footprints than plant-based foods – which typically have ten to fifty times lower emissions compared to similar animal products.[25] As such, eating more plant-based food in place of animal products could reduce the carbon emissions from your food by 90 percent or more.

Other factors that people often focus on to reduce the carbon footprint of their diets, like eating local to reduce the transportation distance of food, typically have far less influence compared to the overall type of food consumed. For example, the carbon footprint associated with the transportation of beef is less than 1 percent of beef's total emissions. So, buying locally produced beef might only shave a tiny amount of the emissions. Overall, the carbon footprint associated with transporting food only accounts for around 6 percent of the emissions from a typical diet, whereas meat, dairy, and eggs account for about 83 percent.[26] So, while eating locally could slightly reduce emissions, changing the composition of your diet is a far more significant factor in lowering your diet's carbon footprint. Instead of focusing too much on food transportation, replacing consumption of animal products with plant-based products is one of the biggest ways to reduce greenhouse gases associated with your diet.

Although the transportation of food isn't a large factor in a typical person's carbon footprint, personal transportation methods are. In fact, personal transportation is one of the largest sources of individual carbon emissions. Why does your personal transportation have such a larger carbon impact compared to the transportation of your food? Personal vehicles are often designed for comfort, frequently carrying just one passenger, whereas cargo vehicles are designed for efficiency, often hauling tons of goods at a time. For the same reason that carpooling is better for the environment, transporting hundreds of thousands of food items at a time results in a small carbon impact per item. In comparison, commercial transportation of food products is far more efficient than personal transportation, pound for pound.

Personal transportation accounts for approximately 25 percent of an individual's carbon footprint, making it one of the largest contributors to greenhouse gas emissions.[27] One simple strategy for reducing emissions from personal transportation is to cut back on total travel miles. This can be done by moving closer to work to reduce commuting miles or by taking fewer long-distance trips. Another important strategy is to improve your travel methods.

Some methods of transportation are far more carbon-intensive than others. Flying and driving gas/diesel cars are among the most carbon-intensive modes of travel. In contrast, public transportation, like trains, subways, and buses, are among the lowest. Of course, walking and biking, when possible, are the most environmentally friendly options, as they produce no direct carbon emissions. Domestic flights emit around 2.5 times the greenhouse gases per mile compared to taking the bus; they also emit over 7 times more than taking a train. Switching to an electric car rather than a gas car can reduce emissions by 70 percent. Taking the train rather than flying or driving can reduce emissions by over 80 percent.[28]

So, in summary, the main advice for reducing your transportation emissions is to (1) reduce overall travel distances and (2) choose more efficient and greener travel methods. As a rule of thumb, walking and biking are best, public transportation is in the middle, and cars and planes are the worst. If driving, smaller vehicles are better than larger ones, and electric cars are better than gas-powered ones.[29] By switching to more efficient modes of transportation and reducing total distances traveled, individuals can significantly reduce their greenhouse gas emissions, contributing to global efforts to mitigate climate change.

The largest category for individual carbon footprints is home energy use, accounting for around 35 percent of an average individual's carbon footprint in the United States.[30] Most of the carbon footprint from home energy use comes from heating and cooling. Space heating alone accounts for 42 percent of household energy consumption, followed by water heating at 18 percent. Air-conditioning accounts for 9 percent and refrigeration around 4 percent. In total, heating accounts for 60 percent of home energy use, while cooling and refrigeration account for 13 percent. Lighting is only 3 percent, and all other appliances combined are only 23 percent.[31] So, if you want to focus on the biggest ways to reduce home energy use, first target heating and cooling systems, which comprise 73 percent of household energy consumption.

An easy, low-cost way to reduce home heating and AC use is to adjust your thermostat to keep the house warmer in summer and cooler in winter. This can be done automatically with programmable or smart thermostats that sense occupancy. Upgrading efficiency is another option that costs more upfront but often saves money in the long run, while reducing GHG emissions. This includes upgrades like better insulation and more efficient appliances, especially heating units, water heaters, and air conditioning. For example, upgrading to a heat pump can reduce heating energy use by 65–80 percent.[32] Another option is switching to renewable energy sources like solar panels. Although they can be expensive to install upfront, solar panel systems can dramatically reduce or even eliminate your reliance on nonrenewable home energy.

In addressing climate change, it's good to recognize the value of individual efforts in reducing carbon footprints through lifestyle changes, especially when focused on the big areas of home energy use, food, and personal travel. As we have seen, focusing on your biggest sources of emissions makes it possible to reduce your individual carbon footprint significantly. Yet, we must be cautious not to overstate the impact of these personal actions. Our individual efforts, while meaningful, are not sufficient to tackle the overarching causes of climate change. As we'll explore in the next section, there is a risk that too much focus on individual lifestyle changes can lead to more harm than good.

4.5 Moral licensing: The danger of sweating the small stuff

A significant danger of focusing on low-impact strategies rather than high-impact ones is moral licensing. Moral licensing, as William MacAskill describes in his book *Doing Good Better*, is the psychological tendency in which people who perform good actions often compensate by doing fewer good deeds in the future.[33] Some studies show that after completing even minor good deeds, people become less likely to engage in further good actions later, perhaps reasoning that they have "done their good deed for the day." For example, in one experiment, students gave less money to charity after committing two hours to help a foreign student study for class.[34] In another experiment, participants were more likely to lie and steal after making an eco-friendly purchase.[35] Although there is continued debate on how much moral licensing influences our decisions,[36] perhaps reflecting on your own behavior, you might remember times when you chose a more self-indulgent action as a reward for a good deed or decided not to participate in further good actions because you have "already done your part."

In many cases, moral licensing is inconsequential. If you do one less small good deed after making a good choice, the world is no worse off. Rewarding yourself after taking extraordinarily good actions could encourage you to continue to do good actions in the future. However, moral licensing can lead to a worse world if you choose not to do a more impactful good deed as a result of your small deeds.

In practice, moral licensing can be net harmful if the time and energy spent on small ways to make a difference make you less likely to take higher-impact actions later on. For example, suppose that George chooses to radically reduce his energy use from lighting. He only uses natural daylight when possible, ensuring all lights are off at night outside his current room, and upgrades all his lightbulbs to more efficient LEDs. In doing so, George estimates he can reduce his lighting energy use by 90 percent. But then, to reward himself after a successful day of light reduction, he treats himself to an extra serving of meat, perhaps a beef burger, with his dinner. Unfortunately, this single meal would likely undo that entire day's GHG reduction from his lighting efforts, due to the high carbon footprint of beef. Later that month, George decides not to invest in home efficiency upgrades since he feels he is already doing his part with his extreme lighting reductions.

But lighting only accounts for around 3 percent of home energy use, so even if George spent his whole life in the dark, he has only reduced his home energy use by a small amount, while becoming less likely to take more significant actions. If spending time upgrading lightbulbs results in not upgrading your old heating system to more efficient models, it could mean more greenhouse gases in the atmosphere overall.

Sweating the small stuff runs the risk of reducing your actions on bigger, higher-impact changes needed to address the root of the climate crisis. When it comes to combating climate change, focusing on greener lifestyle changes might be sweating the small stuff, given the much more significant ways we can influence systemic change. If, after great time and effort, an average American cuts their emissions in half, they would still have a carbon footprint higher than the global average. Moreover, for an average American to reach a sustainable level of emissions through lifestyle changes alone, they would need to reduce their footprint by nearly 90 percent, requiring radical lifestyle changes. In 2021, individuals emitted around 18 tons of greenhouse gases (CO_2e) in the United States, compared to the global average of around 7 tons,[37] while the sustainable target to reach by 2050 is fewer than 2 tons per person annually.[38]

Focusing too much on individual greener lifestyle changes could make us fall victim to moral licensing by not taking the more significant actions necessary to solve climate change. Overprioritizing lifestyle changes presents a moral hazard if it prevents us from taking higher-impact actions. As such, we should be careful in overemphasizing personal lifestyle changes, as this could distract us from taking more effective actions, such as advocating for systemic changes and giving to high-impact climate organizations.

This isn't to say we shouldn't try to make minor improvements in addition to big ones, but that we must keep moral licensing in mind. We should be aware of the danger that small, feel-good actions can distract from higher-impact actions. Nonetheless, lifestyle changes can play a complementary role as long as individuals guard against moral licensing. Living

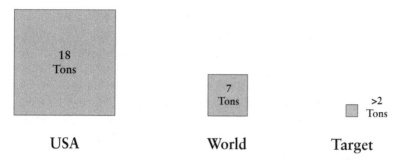

Figure 4.2: Average annual greenhouse gas emissions per person (2021)
Source: Author's figure based on Hannah Ritchie, Pablo Rosado, and Max Roser, "Greenhouse Gas Emissions," *Our World in Data* (January 2024).

more sustainably can help you become a better advocate for climate action and contribute to fostering a climate-conscious culture. To avoid the pitfalls of moral licensing, it is important to focus our time and energy on the biggest, highest-impact actions within our power. At the same time, we don't want to take warnings about moral licensing too far and use them as an excuse to avoid making any greener lifestyle changes, as they can still have value. However, as we have seen, to make the biggest impact on climate change, effective altruists advise that our priority should be taking actions to support and enable systemic transformation through greener policy and innovation.

4.6 Signs for hope: Optimistic changemakers

After decades of hearing scientists raising alarms about the catastrophic consequences of climate change, and year after year of record-breaking temperatures and extreme weather events, it's easy to succumb to "climate doomerism" – the view that climate catastrophe is inevitable, so why should we bother to act. However, as we have seen, there are tangible actions we can take to help solve climate change and reduce its impacts. Succumbing to climate defeatism is dangerous because it leads to inaction which, in turn, guarantees catastrophic results. Just because things will get worse if we do nothing doesn't mean there is nothing we can do. As we have seen throughout this chapter, there are many effective actions that are within our power. Effective altruists tend to argue against doom and gloom approaches, instead highlighting how we can contribute to existing solutions or help develop new ones.

Hannah Ritchie, whose research informed much of this chapter, calls this idea the "optimistic changemakers" approach.[39] She advocates looking for ways to make the future better and acknowledging that it is possible to achieve this through our actions. However, optimism itself can be dangerous if it leads to complacency under the assumption that things will inevitably improve of their own accord. Optimistic changemakers instead choose to envision a realistically better future and look for ways to be part of that change through concrete actions. This involves researching what high-impact actions are available to us, taking some of those actions, and helping inform others of them.

Although there is still much work to be done on climate change, there are plenty of signs of hope. Since the early years of this century, emissions have steadily declined in many areas of the world, including the United States and Europe.[40] As explored in this chapter, the prices of scalable green technologies like wind and solar continue to fall. Large policy victories, like the multibillion-dollar US 2022 Climate Bill, show that change is possible, especially through collective effort focused on systemic solutions.

Just as no single person created the climate crisis, no single person can solve it either. Guided by the systems they live in, billions of people have contributed to global warming through their energy usage, transportation methods, food consumption, and more. Climate change is a problem created by the collective actions of billions of people over decades. So, it follows that it will take the collective action of billions, working together on systemic solutions, to address the problem. By looking for ways we can be part of solutions rather than the problem, we can join the global effort that is already shifting the trajectory of our climate's future. There are many ways to contribute, including supporting systemic policy changes, donating to effective organizations, adopting greener lifestyle habits, and fostering a culture of climate awareness and action.

In addition to giving green and living green, some find that the best way they can make a difference is by devoting their careers to developing and expanding climate solutions. The next chapter explores this approach, of seeking high-impact careers, alongside another global problem that, much like climate change, poses grave risks for humanity – the ever-present threat of nuclear war.

Questions for reflection

1. What role do you think carbon offsets should play, if any, in addressing climate change? How do the challenges of leakage, non-additionality, and non-permanence in carbon offset programs affect your perspective on their role in climate action?
2. Do you think individuals should view investments in climate action rather than direct ways to eliminate their carbon footprint? Why, or why not? Which carbon removal or emissions reduction program do you think is the best approach in the long term? Explain your reasoning.
3. From an effective altruist perspective, how much do you think people should give to high-impact climate charities compared to other charities?
4. If you could enact laws related to climate change, what specific policies would you implement? Focus on policies that could drive system-wide changes and explain their potential impact.

5. Reflecting on the options explored in this chapter, what actions do you find most feasible and impactful for yourself to take now and in the future to combat climate change effectively?
6. How can we guard against moral licensing in our efforts to address climate change? What is the right balance between focusing on greener lifestyles and supporting systemic change?

Classroom exercise

In small groups, first explore the current recommended climate charities from Giving Green, an effective altruist organization, reading over summaries about their strategies and evidence of effectiveness: https://www.givinggreen.earth/top-climate-change-nonprofit-donations-recommendations. Next, discuss which organization you think seems most promising for having the highest impact on climate change. What do you think is the best climate charity to support right now and why? Share your group's pick and rationale. Afterward, vote as a class for the most promising climate nonprofit. Tally the votes and discuss the results.

Helpful resources

Effective altruism and climate change

Michael Townsend, "Is Climate Change the World's Biggest Problem? And What Can We Do About It?" This is an accessible summary of a larger report by John Halstead and Johannes Ackva. *Giving What We Can.* https://www.givingwhatwecan.org/climate-change.

Kara Hunt, "Four Lessons from Effective Altruism That We Can Apply to Climate Change," *Clean Air Task Force.*

https://www.catf.us/2022/07/four-lessons-from-effective-altruism-that-we-can-apply-to-climate-change/.

Climate giving

"Give to High-Impact Climate Nonprofits," *Giving Green*. https://www.givinggreen.earth/top-climate-change-nonprofit-donations-recommendations.

Johannes Ackva, Luisa Sandkühler, and Violet Buxton-Walsh, "Guide to the Changing Landscape of Climate Philanthropy," *Founders Pledge*. https://www.founderspledge.com/research/changing-landscape.

Moral licensing

Lindsay Dodgson, "Here's What 'Moral Licensing' Means," *Business Insider*. https://www.businessinsider.com/what-moral-licensing-means-2017-11.

Irene Blanken, Niels van de Ven, and Marcel Zeelenberg, "A Meta-Analytic Review of Moral Licensing," *Personality and Social Psychology* 41 (no. 4). https://journals.sagepub.com/doi/10.1177/0146167215572134.

Understanding climate change science and data

Hannah Ritchie, Pablo Rosado, and Max Roser, "CO_2 and Greenhouse Gas Emissions," *Our World in Data*. https://ourworldindata.org/co2-and-greenhouse-gas-emissions.

"Carbon Offsets and Carbon Removals Research," *Giving Green*. https://www.givinggreen.earth/carbon-offsets-removals.

Hannah Ritchie, "Climate Change: Turning Down the Thermostat," in *Not the End of the World: How We Can Be the First Generation to Build a Sustainable Planet*. New York: Little, Brown Spark, 2024, Ch. 3.

5

Can Your Career Save the World? Nuclear Weapons and Existential Risk

Your career path is likely one of the most impactful decisions you make, shaping not just your life but the lives of many others. Over the past century, through the work of many individuals' careers, humanity created a technology that has a destructive force beyond anything we previously could imagine: nuclear weapons. As long as nuclear weapons exist, the world will need to make continuous efforts to reduce the risk of nuclear war.

The existence of nuclear weapons is a stark reminder of the momentous impacts our careers can make on the world. In fact, nuclear war is just one example of the existential risks humanity faces, risks with the potential to end or severely curtail human civilization as we know it. Many people have used their professions to help prevent nuclear war and other existential catastrophes.

Throughout this chapter, we'll explore nuclear risk and the broader concept of existential risks. We'll examine how individuals can work to mitigate catastrophic risks through their professional lives and introduce helpful tools and frameworks for using your occupation to make a positive difference. As we will see, you can have a huge impact on the world through your career.

5.1 Using your 80,000 hours

Your most precious and finite resource is time. You only have so many hours in your lifespan; how you spend that time will define your fulfillment in life and your impact on the world. One common way of doing good with your time is volunteering to help local charities. In an increasingly interconnected world, it is also possible, if you have the right skill sets, to volunteer your time online to support charities on the other side of the planet. However, one of the most significant and valuable chunks of time in our lifespan are the decades we devote to our careers.

Individuals typically spend around 80,000 hours of their life in their careers.[1] By leveraging these hours to improve the world, you have an opportunity to make a massive impact. Recognizing the potential of our careers, Benjamin Todd and William MacAskill founded one of the earliest effective altruist organizations, 80,000 Hours. This nonprofit helps individuals improve the positive impact of their career paths. People often spend years preparing for their careers, such as pursuing college degrees. Not many of them devote a significant amount of time in researching which career would be best in terms of its impact on the world. 80,000 Hours helps address this gap by offering guidance in career selection, skill building, and career path improvement so as to make a bigger impact with your time.

One indirect way to use your 80,000 hours to improve the world is through earning to give, as highlighted in Chapter 2 of this book. Anyone can make a significant impact through their occupation by donating a portion of their income to high-impact charities. If you seek higher-paying jobs or promotions so that you can donate more, you can significantly scale your positive impact. However, this is only one of many ways a person can use their career to improve the world. 80,000 Hours promotes earning to give as just one of many high-impact career pathways. Some of the other ways that we will explore later in this chapter include high-impact research, communication and advocacy, organization building, and governmental policy work.

Finding the best avenues to benefit the world involves exploring and investigating the many options where you are especially well-suited to make a difference. 80,000 Hours calls this your personal fit – the probability that you will excel at a job, given your skills, interests, and values.[2] Personal fit is an important factor to consider when choosing a career path, as it can greatly affect your job performance and satisfaction and, as a result, your long-term impact on the world. However, personal fit is not easy to predict in practice. We are often wrong about what we will or won't excel at and enjoy doing, so it requires experimentation and feedback to discover.[3]

Additionally, assessing your potential impact through different career paths or opportunities also matters. One tool that 80,000 Hours recommends using to do so is the scale, neglectedness, and solvability (SNS) framework, which we introduced in Chapter 1. How good would it be for the world if you were successful in a particular career? How much work is already being done on the issue you would be working on? And how likely are you to be successful in that specific career path?[4] These are all important questions to consider when thinking about your future or potential career path changes. In practice, these are complex questions to answer; they are highly individualized, differing from person to person. Not all careers fit every individual's personality, skill set, and life goals. It is helpful to explore your options and, alongside these, carefully weigh up your personal strengths, interests, and values when assessing which career avenues will allow you to best benefit the world with your 80,000 hours.

Another important consideration, according to 80,000 Hours, is how opportunities can help you build career capital. Career capital is anything that helps put you in a better position to have a higher impact later in life.[5] Although some opportunities won't be very impactful in the near term, they could help you to build the tools that will enable you to have a far greater impact in the future than you would have otherwise – tools such as knowledge, connections, reputation, skills, resources, credentials, and virtuous character traits. Some common ways of gaining career capital include college degrees, certifications, and apprenticeships.

By devoting significant time to carefully exploring how to improve your career impact, you'll be better positioned to make a much larger difference with your most precious resource – time. Without careful reflection and research, you could very easily underutilize this massive resource, and what's worse, you risk missing the ways your career could be harmful to the world, which could compound enormous harm over the course of 80,000 hours.

One area that highlights how impactful a career can be to the world, for better or worse, is nuclear security. In the next section, we'll explore the nature of nuclear risk and how individuals have used their careers in the past to make a massive impact in reducing that risk, potentially saving the world.

5.2 The doomsday machine: The ever-present danger of nuclear weapons

One striking example of an individual making an enormous impact through their career is Stanislav Petrov. On September 26, 1983, Soviet early warning systems showed five intercontinental ballistic missiles (ICBMs) launching from the United States toward the Soviet Union. Stanislav Petrov was the duty officer crewing the command bunker for this satellite-based early warning system, and it was his job to report any detected launches to his superiors. This was during a time of heightened tensions between the Soviet Union and the United States during the Cold War. Petrov saw the alarm on the screens and was aware of the real possibility of this leading to a devastating nuclear war with the United States. He thought it was unlikely that the United States would attack the Soviet Union with only five ICBMs but he had no evidence to suggest this was a false alarm. Given the stakes, Petrov decided to report this as a false alarm to his superiors, even though he was still uncertain. It was discovered much later that this was indeed a false alarm caused by an extremely rare alignment of the sun, clouds, the detection satellite, and the US missile fields they were monitoring. Still, Petrov had no way of knowing this at the time.[6]

Petrov's decision to report this as a false alarm potentially saved the world from nuclear war. This is because decisions on whether to launch a retaliatory nuclear strike must be made quickly, due to the speed of ICBMs. As missile technology advances, their nuclear payload delivery speed increases, which shortens the time decision-makers have on whether to launch a nuclear counterstrike. The window of time nations have to mount a counterstrike is now down to well under thirty minutes, and the practical decision window is only a handful of minutes.[7] In the United States, once a president orders a nuclear counterstrike, missiles fire within just a few minutes, with no way to reverse the launch command.[8] Once a nation receives an alarm of a potential incoming nuclear strike, they only have minutes in which to review the information, assess how credible the threat is, and make a decision whether to mount a counterstrike – just a few minutes to decide the fate of the world.

Given the speed at which countries can mount a nuclear strike, a common nuclear weapons strategy is called "launch on warning." Since nuclear strategists would likely target the opposing country's nuclear launch capabilities with their initial strikes, if a nation wants to mount a retaliatory strike, it must do so while the initial attack missiles are still in the air. This launch on warning strategy is a central component of the theory of Mutually Assured Destruction (MAD).

MAD theory claims that nuclear-armed countries are less likely to attack each other, since both sides can retaliate with utter destruction. According to MAD, the reward for building and maintaining a nuclear arsenal is that it deters attacks from other nuclear-armed countries. Due to this deterrent effect, some scholars claim that nuclear weapons have reduced large-scale global warfare; large global powers no longer wage direct warfare with each other, as it would result in their own destruction. For example, in the Russia–Ukraine war that began in 2022, the United States and the European Union have both heavily funded Ukraine's resistance and supplied them with weapons, but have been very careful not to directly participate in the war by sending troops. In a world without nuclear weapons, the United States and the European Union would likely have played a much more direct role in defending Ukraine, resulting in a much larger global conflict and potentially another world war.

Whether MAD has reduced violent warfare between nations overall or moved these conflicts into proxy wars where battles are fought in different ways is a matter of debate. However, this helps explain why many countries spend enormous resources to develop and maintain their own nuclear weapons programs – they believe in some version of MAD theory, namely that it helps deter other countries from directly attacking them.

Nine nuclear-armed countries collectively hold more than 12,000 nuclear warheads (Russia, United States, China, France, United Kingdom, Pakistan, India, Israel, and North Korea). Russia and the United States have the vast majority of them, around 88 percent, more than 5,000 each. More than 3,800 nuclear weapons stand at the ready on missiles or on bomber bases, many aimed at strategic targets across the globe, with around 2,000 of those set on high alert.[9] These nuclear stockpiles are maintained, updated, and continually developed in large part because of mutually assured destruction theory. By participating in the MAD approach, the United States, Russia, and other nuclear powers have created what Daniel Ellsberg, a former nuclear war planner, called a "doomsday machine." If anything goes wrong with this globally maintained mechanism, it could easily result in the destruction of our world.[10]

Researchers warn that even a relatively small nuclear exchange between two countries, such as between India and Pakistan, could result in a devastating global nuclear winter, threatening worldwide mass starvation.[11] This doomsday scenario that humanity created and continues to maintain endangers not only the countries involved in a nuclear exchange but all life on the planet. Shockingly, this global doomsday machine has been on the verge of being accidentally activated on many occasions. Stanislav Petrov's example is not the only close call the world has faced – there have been many, many others. Our World in Data has documented more than a dozen close calls from 1957 to 2007,[12] and these are only the cases we currently know of; there could be many others that have yet to be uncovered or declassified. Each of these cases could easily have ended the world as we know it.

Given the danger it poses for all of humanity, nuclear risk is different from many of the other problems explored in this book so far. It is an example of a frightening category of risks involving the largest possible scale, existential risks, which we'll explore in the next section.

5.3 Existential risks

Existential risks are threats that could lead to human extinction or otherwise severely limit our long-term potential. The Swedish philosopher Nick Bostrom introduced the term in 2002 and has devoted much of his career to researching and writing on the topic.[13] He notes that existential risks are different from those we are accustomed to and he explains why by categorizing risks based on their scope and severity. The scope of risks could be personal, local, regional, or global; each of these can have varying severities, from survivable to terminal. For example, your risk of death in a car crash is a personal terminal risk, whereas a worldwide recession is an example of a global survivable risk. Existential risks have the highest possible scope and severity – these are global terminal risks. Due to the immense scale of these risks, many effective altruists choose to work on preventing existential catastrophes.

Existential risks threaten everything – all that is valuable about the human experience and all the achievements that humanity has cultivated up to this point. Since existential risks threaten human extinction, not only do they risk the lives of all those living today, around 8 billion people, but they also risk the lives of all future generations – either by preventing them from ever being born or by creating permanent conditions severely limiting their potential. If an existential catastrophe occurred, we would no longer pass down anything we value to our grandchildren, great-grandchildren, or other distant descendants of humanity. In such a case, nothing we love about the human experience would be passed onward to be cherished and cared for by others.

With the technological achievement of unlocking the power of the atom, we have created the possibility of nuclear war for all future generations. As long as we can create nuclear weapons and nuclear arsenals are maintained, this existential threat remains. However, nuclear war is just one of many existential risks. These risks are grouped into two main categories: natural and anthropogenic (human-created).

Scientists have long known of natural existential risks, as there have been many mass extinction events in Earth's past. One such example is the asteroid impact that led to the extinction of the dinosaurs and most of life on Earth. Thankfully, scientists have identified the majority of large asteroids in our region of the solar system, through tracking and monitoring systems, and found that they do not pose any significant risk to humanity over the next century.[14] Super-volcanoes are another naturally occurring existential risk responsible for mass global extinction events in Earth's past. Fortunately, super-volcanic eruptions large enough to threaten human extinction are extremely rare. Although scientists view a super-volcanic eruption as extremely unlikely at any time in the near future, we know little about how to predict them or stop them from happening. As a result, they remain a concern.[15]

Natural extinction risks are inherent to all living species, past and present. Humans uniquely face self-created technological dangers. The doomsday machine that we have created from nuclear weapons is just one of many risks we face through our technological innovation, as we will explore in the next section.

5.4 On the precipice: Anthropogenic risks

As we continue to innovate and create more powerful technologies, we open up the possibility of other unforeseen catastrophic consequences of future technologies. In addition to nuclear war, other examples of potential anthropogenic (human-created) existential risks are engineered pandemics, climate change, and unaligned artificial intelligence. Advances in biotechnology are making it possible to engineer extremely dangerous pathogens. This could lead to weaponization or unintentional lab leaks of "superbugs," risking far more lethal and contagious pandemics than we have ever faced from natural diseases. Concerning climate change, if world events cause us to reverse our progress on decarbonization, in worst-case scenarios, a runaway greenhouse effect could make the world uninhabitable. As we'll explore in the next chapter, future advanced artificial intelligence could surpass our own intellect and power, escaping our control.

We live in an age of elevated existential risks due to the unintended consequences of our technological advancement. The philosopher Toby Ord calls this "the precipice," which he defines as the age of heightened existential risk due to human actions. Ord invites us to imagine that humanity is currently on the brink of a precipice, the edge of a cliff. After a long and arduous journey through the wilderness, there is no way backward; the only way forward is along this dangerous precipice. If we fall, we lose everything. But if humanity makes it through this perilous portion of human history, future generations can take advantage of all that technological innovation has to offer. If we survive the precipice, Ord imagines a future in which we could use technology to solve the world's most pressing problems, allowing future generations to flourish. He characterizes our current age as having the potential for disaster but also the potential for a prosperous future. As such, he describes our present age, living on the precipice, as having an opportunity for great meaning and purpose by guiding humanity through this moment of heightened risk and extreme stakes.[16]

Ord marks the beginning point of the precipice with the Trinity Test – the first detonation of a nuclear weapon as part of the Manhattan Project on July 16, 1945. Early in the development of the first atomic bomb, scientists raised concerns that a nuclear fission explosion could result in a chain reaction that would ignite the atmosphere. This atmospheric ignition would cascade into a fireball, engulfing the entire planet. Concerned by this, scientists on the Manhattan Project conducted studies and determined that atmospheric ignition was extremely unlikely, although they could not rule out the possibility entirely. When it came to nuclear technology, they were in uncharted waters; practical tests don't always line up with theoretical physics. Even though the risk of atmospheric ignition could not be ruled out, the Trinity Test went forward, detonating the first atomic bomb.[17]

Luckily, the Trinity Test did not ignite the atmosphere and end all of life. However, the dice were rolled, risking the planet with the development of nuclear weapons, not only with the initial Trinity Test but also through the current doomsday machine that humanity maintains with its nuclear arsenals. This is why Ord marks the Trinity Test as the beginning of the age of the precipice – the beginning of the era of humans risking their own extinction through the development of powerful technologies.[18]

Given this age of heightened risk due to our own devices, how can we reduce existential risk so that humanity can navigate through the precipice and onward to a more prosperous and safe future? The following section explores a variety of approaches individuals can take to help reduce existential risk through their careers.

5.5 Reducing existential risk: Four approaches

To ensure humanity's survival and a safer future for the world, we need to find ways to mitigate existential risks. Working on this could be one of the most impactful things a person could do with their career. But given their scale, how do we go about reducing these risks? Benjamin Todd, from 80,000 Hours, has outlined several general approaches, which fall under four categories: targeted efforts, broad-scope efforts, capacity building, and investigation.[19] Let's go over each and see how they could apply to reducing existential risk in general and nuclear risk in particular.

The first approach is targeted efforts. This approach attempts to address identified existential risks head-on. Given their scale and severity, we need to devote significant effort and resources to reducing existential risks once they are identified. When existential risks, such as nuclear war, are discovered, we need people to work directly on policies, technologies, and systems that will help prevent these risks from wiping out humanity. Applying this approach to reducing nuclear risk could involve working to shrink nuclear stockpiles, improving nuclear command and control systems, preventing nuclear proliferation, and advocating for risk-reducing policies such as no-first-use doctrines.

The next approach is working on broad-scope efforts. This involves strategies that can apply to multiple existential threats simultaneously. This means not just concentrating on preventing nuclear war but also developing methods that can help safeguard against other threats at the same time, such as engineered pandemics or artificial intelligence. For example, developing and implementing strategies that reduce the escalation of large power conflicts could help reduce the proliferation and development of a wide range of dangerous technologies, helping to safeguard against nuclear war but also other existential risks like bio-weapons and weaponized AI. This could involve improving foreign relations, global cooperation, peace-building, and strengthening international institutions.

Another avenue for broad-scope efforts is developing "plan B" strategies that help humanity survive catastrophic events. The goal is to maximize the probability of an okay outcome, what Bostrom calls the "maxipok" strategy, where humanity can recover from worst-case scenarios.[20] This could involve developing plans for shelters, seed vaults, and alternative food sources, all of which could help humanity rebound from catastrophic events rather than go extinct.

A third approach is called capacity building. Capacity building involves building, supporting, or advocating for communities and organizations that focus on reducing existential risk. This could include creating or joining movements, groups, networks, nonprofits, or other organizations with a common goal of reducing existential risks. For example, an effort to reduce nuclear risk could involve founding organizations that aim to reduce the risk of a nuclear disaster or promote peace-building. This could also involve working for or supporting existing organizations such as the Nuclear Threat Initiative, the Future of Life Institute, the Carnegie Endowment for International Peace, the International Peace Museum, and the Nuclear Age Peace Foundation.

A fourth approach is investigation, which involves discovering more about existential risks. This approach consists of conducting rigorous research to increase our understanding of existential risks and how to prevent them. This work could involve investigating existential risks broadly or narrowly, such as global priorities research, studying the impacts of new technologies, and evaluating the effectiveness of various risk mitigation strategies. Applying this approach to reducing nuclear risk could involve researching the nature and magnitude of nuclear conflict, investigating the implications of new nuclear technologies, and researching nuclear strategies to determine which ones reduce risk the most.

In addition to being helpful strategies for mitigating existential risk, there are many careers that help implement these four approaches to help solve a variety of world problems. Depending on how these approaches align with your personal fit, there are many potential high-impact career paths to choose from, which we'll explore next.

5.6 Reducing nuclear risk: Five high-impact career paths

In the 80,000 Hours career guide, Benjamin Todd explores ways in which people can find impactful and fulfilling careers. The highest-impact career paths often fall into five main categories: governmental policy work, research, communications, building organizations, and supporting roles such as earning to give.[21] These types of careers can help reduce existential risk, but they could also be high-impact career paths for those seeking to help solve any of the large global problems explored in this book. Often, many of the best ways to use your career to make a difference fall within one of these categories, no matter what problems you choose to devote your time to working on. Although this list is not meant to be exhaustive, it can aid in thinking about career plans and how you can best use your career to benefit the world. Let's go over each of these career paths and see how they could apply to reducing nuclear risk.

One category of high-impact careers is government and policy work. This involves working with or influencing the public sector, helping shape the policies and strategies that could potentially impact entire communities, nations, or even the world, depending on the level of government. Some examples of careers in this category that could help reduce nuclear risk include politicians, diplomats, defense and intelligence analysts, and congressional staffers. Government and policy work could help improve international coordination and high-stakes decision-making, as well as prevent conflicts that could escalate into nuclear war.

Another potentially high-impact career path is research. These careers involve rigorously studying problems to help develop and improve potential solutions. Many of the highest-impact people in history have been researchers who made enormous discoveries or developed important ideas into practical solutions. Current pressing world problems either do not have solutions or need better ones that are more scalable and efficient to address problems more quickly. Those wanting to take this approach to reduce nuclear risk could do so in many careers, ranging from university academics to think-tank researchers to scientists and engineers. Some research areas include developing technologies that can help safeguard, prevent, or identify false alarms of nuclear strikes and helping research nuclear policies and strategies to reduce the likelihood of nuclear catastrophe. Researchers can also perform important work that can help inform other high-impact careers, such as government and policy work.

Once helpful strategies or solutions are discovered, researchers often need help spreading those ideas, which leads us to the next high-impact career path: communications careers. Communication is a broad category of careers, including jobs like educators, activists, content creators, journalists, and many other jobs in media such as radio, TV, newspapers, and entertainment. Skillful communicators can help spread important ideas to a wide range of audiences, including important leaders, to help inform and improve decision-making regarding world problems. This is a flexible role that could be pursued as a full-time job or in an individual's spare time, such as through participating in events organized by activists. There are many communication career paths that can help raise awareness and understanding of current risks associated with nuclear warfare and how others can help reduce those risks. An effective communicator could convince many more individuals to work on problems like reducing nuclear risk, potentially making much more of an impact, compared to if they worked on those problems directly. However, there is a danger with this approach in that poor communicators could cause more harm than good by spreading misinformation or leading people down the wrong path.

Another potential high-impact career path is organization building. This approach involves helping to start and run nonprofits that directly address problems. In many cases, the highest impact nonprofits are the organizations working on highly neglected issues or doing work that no other organizations currently focus on. You could look for gaps where there is little work being done on important issues, then help start and sustain a new nonprofit to address them. Building and maintaining a successful new nonprofit organization is difficult work, but it can be highly impactful, especially when filling current gaps in problem-solving. One organization that helps people explore this career path is Charity Entrepreneurship – a nonprofit that aims to help potential founders refine their ideas, gain training, and potentially receive funding when ready. Hopefully, with more effective charities helping solve the world's most pressing problems, solutions will be found and implemented sooner.

Last but not least are supporting roles, our final main category of high-impact career paths. This career path involves attempting to support any of the above high-impact work of others. You could do this indirectly through donating funds, such as through earning to give, as explored in Chapter 2. Another more direct option is to seek a career working in a support position, assisting high-impact individuals or organizations. As such, this career path can take many forms, including administrators, grant-makers, assistants, managers, and productivity coaches.

Regarding nuclear risk, this could involve earning to give by seeking high-income jobs so you could donate more to organizations working on reducing nuclear risk. Another option is taking the Giving What We Can pledge, committing to give 10 percent or more of your income to high-impact charities. Giving What We Can manages a "Risks and Resilience Fund," which could be a good opportunity for those wanting to devote a portion of their donations to reducing catastrophic risks such as nuclear warfare. Other more direct supporting positions could involve working as an assistant, grant-maker, or administrator for nuclear security organizations.

These are just some examples of how individuals can use their occupations to help solve the world's most pressing problems, including reducing the risk of nuclear disaster. These examples illustrate that, with careful deliberation on your career path, there are many different avenues you can take to make a positive difference through your profession. However, as we'll explore next, it's important to note that there are many objections to the general effective altruist approach to career planning, including objections to focusing your career on reducing existential risk or nuclear risk.

5.7 Objections to devoting your career to nuclear security

First, let's explore a few objections to working on nuclear risk. Then, we'll go over a couple more objections to focusing on existential risk more broadly. Examining these objections and potential responses to them will help us better understand the challenging considerations involved in choosing a career path dedicated to helping solve world problems.

The first objection to focusing on nuclear risk reduction as a career path is the narrow scope of many options in this field, which may not appeal to everyone. When considering careers aimed at mitigating nuclear risk, you might not feel as if you will excel or be passionate enough about the work to truly thrive in one of those career paths. The most promising career paths for reducing the risk of nuclear war involve working in government, the military, or conducting rigorous and narrow academic research. Additionally, many of those careers are highly competitive, making it difficult to achieve a position influential enough to significantly impact nuclear risk reduction. Although there are many types of careers in this area, as outlined in the previous section, they might not be suitable for everyone.

As explored at the beginning of this chapter, personal fit plays an important role in selecting a career path. Individuals are more likely to excel in careers that better suit their skills, values, and character. Picking the right career can not only help individuals obtain more job satisfaction but also help them excel in their jobs in ways they wouldn't have otherwise. As such, personal fit is an important consideration when determining what career path to aim for or pursue. However, it's hard to predict what jobs or careers an individual will genuinely excel at or find fulfilling. Going with your gut is not always the best option for such an important decision about how to use a significant amount of time on this planet.

In the 80,000 Hours career guide, Benjamin Todd advocates not relying solely on your gut but instead thinking like a scientist to predict and assess what careers would be the best personal fit for you.[22] This could involve coming up with hypotheses or best guesses, identifying key uncertainties, and conducting investigations. For example, you could make lists of options and run some cheap and easy tests to see if they are a good fit. You could speak to someone already in that career path, research the job's daily activities, apply for internships, shadow a job, or even take a job temporarily to get exposure to what the work actually involves.

After investigating, you may still conclude that nuclear risk reduction careers aren't the best fit for you. Nonetheless, this is only one of many significant world issues. You could explore many other career options to address other pressing problems.

Another common objection to working on reducing nuclear risk is the claim that it is not a neglected cause area. In this line of objection, some state that nuclear risk already receives a lot of attention, making it less neglected than other large problems. The risk of nuclear war is an issue we've been aware of for generations now, with many individuals spending their entire life researching it. Proposals and strategies have been continually worked on by governments and militaries for decades. Nuclear risk is also a problem that the general public is aware of, with occasional blockbuster movies dedicated to the topic, such as the 2023 award-winning film *Oppenheimer*.

However, many experts are concerned that there is a growing complacency around the current state of nuclear risk and that it still does not receive enough attention and resources, given how enormous the risks are. There is a worry that the resources dedicated to nuclear security are diminishing over time even while the risks remain the same or are heightening. In 2023, the MacArthur Foundation withdrew its funding from nuclear risk reduction – it was the single biggest funder of work in this area. This came at a time of elevated tensions between major nuclear powers, Russia and the United States, due to the war in Ukraine.

The field of nuclear risk reduction receives an estimated $30–50 million of philanthropic funding per year. In comparison, the 2023 *Oppenheimer* film had a budget of over $100 million, two to three times the amount dedicated to nonprofits working on preventing nuclear war.[23] Governments and militaries also dedicate time and resources toward nuclear risk reduction. However, exactly how much government funding goes toward mitigating nuclear risk is unclear.

When risks are at the level of human extinction, it is difficult to assess when the appropriate levels of resources are being dedicated. This leads us to the next objection – questioning whether nuclear war is genuinely an existential risk after all. In *The Precipice*, Ord estimates the chance of an existential catastrophe via nuclear war over the next 100 years to be only one in a thousand.[24] This is because even if a nuclear war causes a nuclear winter, wiping out most of the human population, there will likely still be some areas of the world, such as New

Zealand, that will remain habitable. Humans have survived ice ages in the past without the aid of modern technology, so it seems plausible that humanity would survive a nuclear winter, even if it is the most catastrophic event we have ever faced.

Therefore, those who see reducing existential risk as the highest priority may choose to work on other threats with a higher likelihood of wiping out humanity, such as risks related to engineered pandemics or unaligned artificial intelligence. (According to Ord, the odds of these resulting in an existential catastrophe within the next century are approximately one in thirty for engineered pandemics and one in ten for unaligned AI.)[25] However, there is still much uncertainty in terms of the effects of a large-scale nuclear war. A one in a thousand risk of an existential catastrophe is still an unsettling level of risk for all of humanity, worse odds than dying from activities such as white-water rafting, mountain climbing, paragliding, or sky diving.[26] These are activities that many people find too risky for their own personal comfort. Having this level of extinction risk for all humanity due to nuclear weapons should be even more disconcerting.

5.8 Objections to devoting your career to reducing existential risk

Let's now explore a couple more general objections to working on existential risks as a whole. The first objection concerns human resilience – it's difficult to completely wipe out humanity as long as some populations survive. One of the worst catastrophes in human history was the Black Death pandemic, which killed as many as half of all people in Europe in the fourteenth century. If a worse catastrophe occurred today, wiping out half of all humans across the globe, it would be the largest loss of life in history, but it would only set population levels back to those of the 1970s. If it wiped out 90 percent of the population, it would reduce the world's population levels to that of the late eighteenth century. If the catastrophe were to kill 99 percent of humans, it would bring us back to population levels of around 1000 BC,[27] around the time of the reign of King David in Israel. Presumably, it wouldn't take another 3,000 years to rebuild modern civilization, given our technological advances. As long as some pockets of humanity survive catastrophic events, humankind can rebuild over time. Given this, it is very difficult to cause complete human extinction.

However, when discussing risks associated with new and developing technologies, these are threats humanity has never faced before, so it is uncertain whether any humans would survive or be able to recover from catastrophic events like nuclear war or engineered pandemics. We don't know how bad they would be for the world in practice. These risks might be less severe than we realize, but they could also be much more dangerous. This uncertainty cuts both ways. Although we cannot be certain such catastrophic events would lead to human extinction, that uncertainty also means those events could be far more severe than we currently predict. So-called existential risks might be less severe and less likely to occur than we realize, but they also could be much more imminent and have more dangerous cascading effects than we currently understand. Such is the nature of dealing with uncertain yet powerful new technologies.

This uncertainty makes it very difficult to estimate how effective it is for an individual to work in these cause areas. This leads to our final objection, which explores the difficulty in determining cost-effectiveness when dealing with existential risks. As we have explored previously in this book, one way to estimate cost-effectiveness is to evaluate how much good can be done with additional resources dedicated to a cause – for example, how much money does it take to save a life? As explored in Chapter 2, cause areas like reducing poverty have high expected cost-effectiveness estimates, with some interventions taking as little as $3,500 to save a life. These estimates often rely on tangible evidence like randomized control trials.

However, estimating the cost-effectiveness of existential risk reduction presents numerous challenges. It's difficult to gather clear evidence tied to existential risks, where these risks are so catastrophically large we cannot test them. Estimating the probability of catastrophic events that could result in human extinction is an extremely complex task. Furthermore, knowing when we've succeeded in preventing an existential catastrophe is tricky, as success means things continue as usual; it is also impossible to know for sure how severe a prevented disaster would have been. With existential risk mitigation, we are working to avoid hypothetical scenarios rather than responding to immediate, observable problems. This makes determining impact and cost-effectiveness much more complex and uncertain. This uncertainty makes it hard for individuals to assess whether focusing on existential risks is the best use of their time.

Despite the uncertainties involved, some effective altruists have tried to provide rough cost-effectiveness numbers for existential risk reduction, but these estimates vary widely. Some estimates range as low as $1,000 per life saved, while others are as high as $300,000 per life saved.[28] These estimate the costs of preventing existential catastrophes compared to the benefit of saving the lives of the current world population, around 8 billion people. However, some effective altruists claim that the main benefits of preventing an existential risk are not just that the lives of our current generation are saved but that the lives of all future generations are saved as well. The scaling effect, when considering the benefits to all potential future generations, is something that could make existential risk reduction far more cost-effective than other world problems. (We'll explore considerations surrounding future generations in more detail in the next chapter.)

However, even without including future generations in cost-effectiveness calculations, for most people, reducing the likelihood of catastrophic events seems like an obvious good. Nonetheless, there is a great deal of uncertainty around both the best ways to reduce catastrophic risks and how to compare the benefits of doing so with other ways of doing good in the world. This relates to the general question of solvability and tractability of addressing existential risks. Reducing these risks clearly has a high scale in terms of potential impact, but there is still an open question of just how solvable these problems are, even with more resources devoted to them.

Those working on existential risk reduction must be comfortable with a higher degree of uncertainty than those in other cause areas who may have more confidence in the impact they can make with their time and resources. Nonetheless, many effective altruists agree that whether or not they personally work on existential risk reduction, preventing catastrophic events is a good thing, and, given the increasing risks involved with developing powerful new technologies, humanity is underprioritizing efforts to mitigate these risks.

5.9 Conclusion

This chapter has introduced the notion of existential risks and, in particular, the risk of nuclear war. You may or may not view these risks as among the world's most pressing problems; nonetheless, the ideas presented here aim to provide concepts and frameworks that can help explore ways you might use your career to improve the world, no matter what issues you see as top priorities. The strategies covered, such as investigation and capacity building through careers in government policy, research, and earning to give, are all useful approaches to using your 80,000 hours to do good.

For those who would like to learn more, the organizations 80,000 Hours and Probably Good provide a wealth of resources on their websites and career guides. They also offer one-on-one career advice for those who want guidance on how best to utilize their careers to do good. While this chapter has focused mainly on career advice from 80,000 Hours, Probably Good also provides resources to help individuals navigate high-impact career decisions. The main difference between these two effective altruist organizations is their focus. 80,000 Hours focuses more on reducing existential risk and advocates more for longtermist approaches, though it also provides plenty of guidance on other cause areas. Probably Good focuses more on current global problems like poverty, climate change, and animal welfare, though it still views existential risks as important. Both are great options for those who want to explore further how they can use their careers to improve the world.

Although this chapter has highlighted the concerning nature of nuclear and existential risks, we have come a long way in a short amount of time. When Nick Bostrom first introduced the term in the early 2000s, very little research and resources were devoted to directly reducing existential risks. Two decades later, numerous initiatives and institutes, and millions of dollars, are now dedicated to researching and mitigating existential risks. These include the Centre for the Study of Existential Risk, the Stanford Existential Risk Initiative, existential risk centers at Cambridge and Berkeley, and the Future of Life Institute.

Regarding the specific risk of nuclear weapons, although constant vigilance is still required and more work is needed, we can find some hope in humanity's ability thus far to survive for more than seventy years alongside this extremely risky technology. Studying this topic could give us insight into strategies for survival with increasingly powerful technologies. However, when the stakes are the whole of human civilization, present and future, many effective altruists warn that the resources, attention, and careers devoted to existential risk reduction are still far too low, given the magnitude of the problem.

Nuclear weapons pose a major threat, but they are not the only existential threats we have made or will create in the future. As our technology grows more powerful, we create more potential existential risks; our survival relies on how we handle and respond to these threats. Many experts view the development of what may soon be the most powerful technology humans have invented, artificial intelligence, as one of the greatest existential risks we face over the next century. The next chapter will explore the risks and rewards of AI and what it means for humanity's long-term potential.

Questions for reflection

1. In what ways can you use your own career to benefit the world? Of some of the career options explored in this chapter, which ones are most applicable to you?
2. How great of a risk do you think nuclear war is? How do you think the world can best mitigate this risk? What careers do you think are best suited to help reduce the risk of nuclear war?
3. What do you think is the greatest existential risk facing humanity? What do you think are the best ways to reduce that risk? Are there ways you can use your career to help? Explain.
4. How should we prioritize existential risk reduction compared to other global problems explored in this book, such as global poverty? Do you think existential risks get sufficient attention and resources? Are there some that do not? Explain.

Classroom exercise

In small groups, first take a few minutes to explore some of the career profiles by Probably Good (https://probablygood.org/career-profiles/) and/or 80,000 Hours (https://80000hours.org/career-reviews/). Pick what you think would be the highest-impact career, and which would be most feasible for someone in your group to achieve. Summarize some of the key details from the career profile and present to the class why you think it has the highest potential to do good in the world. Afterward, vote for which of the other options presented would be the highest-impact career. Discuss the results.

Helpful resources

Effective altruism and high-impact careers

Benjamin Hilton, "Summary: How to Find a Fulfilling Career That Does Good," *80,000 Hours*, May 2023. https://80000hours.org/career-guide/summary/.

"Career Guide: How to Do Good with Your Work," *Probably Good*. https://probablygood.org/career-guide/.

Benjamin Todd, *80,000 Hours: Find a Fulfilling Career That Does Good*. Oxford: Trojan House, 2023.

William MacAskill, "Don't 'Follow Your Passion': Which Careers Make the Most Difference?" in *Doing Good Better: How Effective Altruism Can Help You Make a Difference*. New York: Gotham Books, 2015, Ch. 9.

Nuclear risk

Max Roser, "Nuclear Weapons: Why Reducing the Risk of Nuclear War Should Be a Key Concern of Our Generation," *Our World in Data*, March 3, 2022. https://ourworldindata.org/nuclear-weapons-risk.

Benjamin Hilton and Peter McIntyre, "How You Can Lower the Risk of a Catastrophic Nuclear War," *80,000 Hours*, June 2022. https://80000hours.org/problem-profiles/nuclear-security/.

Fred Kaplan, "The Illogic of Nuclear Escalation," *Asterisk* 1, no. 1 (November 2022). https://asteriskmag.com/issues/01/the-illogic-of-nuclear-escalation.

Matt Bivens, "How Worldwide Famine Would Follow Even a 'Limited' Nuclear War," *The Nation*, August 22, 2022. https://www.thenation.com/article/world/how-worldwide-famine-would-follow-even-a-limited-nuclear-war/.

Daniel Ellsberg, *The Doomsday Machine: Confessions of a Nuclear War Planner*. New York: Bloomsbury, 2017.

Existential risk

Benjamin Todd, "The Case for Reducing Existential Risks," *80,000 Hours*, June 2022. https://80000hours.org/articles/existential-risks/.

Toby Ord, "Existential Risk," in *The Precipice: Existential Risk and the Future of Humanity*. New York: Hachette Books, 2020, Ch. 2.

William MacAskill, "Extinction," in *What We Owe the Future*. New York: Hachette Book Group, 2022, Ch. 5.

Nick Bostrom, "Existential Risks: Analyzing Human Extinction Scenarios," *Journal of Evolution and Technology* 9, no. 1 (2002). https://nickbostrom.com/existential/risks.

6

High Risks and Rewards: AI and Longtermism

The more powerful our technology becomes, the more we have the potential to shape the long-term future of humanity, for better or for worse. Our increasing ability to influence the lives of future generations demands careful consideration of the far-reaching impacts our actions today can have. This has led some effective altruists to develop and promote a moral framework called longtermism, which emphasizes the importance of protecting and positively influencing our long-term future.

In this chapter, we will introduce longtermism alongside an exploration of the risks and rewards associated with what may soon become the most powerful technology humanity has ever invented: advanced artificial intelligence (AI). AI has the potential to bring about both immense benefits and catastrophic risks for humanity. On one hand, AI could help us solve global problems, allowing humanity to flourish; on the other, AI could supercharge the development of harmful technologies and surpass us in all capabilities, posing an existential risk to humanity.

This chapter explores the ethical implications that advanced AI could have for our species. As we will see, current debates surrounding the development of AI mirror ongoing debates among effective altruists. These include whether we should delay or accelerate AI development and how much we should focus on near-term global problems compared to long-term challenges affecting future generations. However, before diving into the topics of longtermism and AI in more detail, let's first explore the broader topic of technological risk and its implications for future generations.

6.1 Risking our future: Technological risk and future generations

Our lives today have been transformed by technologies passed down from previous generations. The twentieth century saw the emergence of innovations with immense potential to profoundly shape humanity's trajectory, passing on to the twenty-first century both tremendous benefits and risks. Nuclear technology is a prime example, as explored in the previous chapter. By unlocking the power of the atom, researchers opened the door to many beneficial technologies, such as nuclear energy. Simultaneously, humanity created some of the most significant risks it has ever faced. Beginning with the first detonation of a nuclear weapon in 1945, humanity has been rolling the dice on our collective future, jeopardizing the lives of all future generations.

Similarly, fossil fuel technologies have provided humanity with a massive source of cheap energy, driving tremendous economic growth. But our use of fossil fuels has also led to climate change, creating new challenges for all life on the planet, now and in the future. Another example is biotechnology, where technological advances have offered life-saving vaccines and antibiotics, saving millions. Yet, at the same time, advanced biotechnology also gives us the potential to resurrect devastating diseases such as smallpox or engineer new pathogens far worse than any humanity has faced in the past.

As humanity continues to develop ever more powerful technologies, we must grapple with their far-reaching implications. Both the promise and the perils of rapidly developing technology will impact the future of humanity for generations to come. Careful ethical consideration, responsible innovation frameworks, and long-term planning are crucial to ensuring that the ever more powerful innovations we develop benefit, rather than endanger, humanity. Nick Bostrom provides an analogy, described in Box 6.1, that helps put the risks and rewards of new powerful technology into perspective.

Much like nuclear weaponry, which was one of the defining technologies of the twentieth century, AI now seems poised to be one of the defining technologies of the twenty-first century. Thinkers like Nick Bostrom and Toby Ord argue that AI's potential to profoundly shape humanity's future requires proactive preparation, risk assessment, and mitigation to prevent disasters before they occur. In his book *The Precipice*, Ord estimated the odds of various existential catastrophes occurring over the next century.[1] While risks from natural causes, like asteroids or super-volcanoes, are around one in ten thousand, the threats humanity has created for itself are far more alarming. Ord estimates the odds of an existential catastrophe from nuclear war and climate change are each around one in a thousand, whereas the odds from engineered pandemics are one in thirty. However, Toby Ord sees artificial intelligence as the most significant near-term risk, representing a startling one in ten chance of existential catastrophe within the next one hundred years.

In total, Ord estimated that, as a result of technological innovations, there is a one in six chance that humanity will wipe itself out within the next century. On one level, this implies that humanity is likely to survive. So, an 83 percent chance of surviving the next one hundred years might sound reassuring to some. But this is equivalent to playing Russian roulette with all of life at stake. If Ord's estimates are correct, we have effectively loaded a bullet into a revolver, spun the chamber, and are pulling the trigger pointed at the head of all of humanity. In doing so, we put in mortal danger not only our current generation but all future generations as well.

Some respond to our risk of extinction with a pessimistic outlook, arguing that human extinction might be appropriate

Box 6.1: Nick Bostrom's urn of invention

Throughout most of human history, we have innovated first, dealing with the risks and rewards later. To describe the dangers of this approach to emerging technologies, Nick Bostrom uses an analogy he calls the "urn of invention." Bostrom's urn contains marbles, each one representing possible technological advancements. Some of these marbles are white, representing immensely beneficial technologies with little downside, like many medical and farming innovations. Due to these types of innovations, technology has caused child mortality rates worldwide to plummet from about 50 percent in the 1800s to 4 percent today. While much more work is needed to reduce global mortality rates closer to 0 percent, this highlights technology's immense potential to improve life.

However, most marbles in the urn are various shades of gray, representing a spectrum of risk and reward. Some are very light gray, representing technologies that are largely beneficial but with minor risks; others, in medium shades of gray, come with a balance of risks and rewards, while the darker shades offer some benefits alongside more significant dangers.

Throughout history, humanity has haphazardly drawn marbles from this urn, dealing with the consequences after the fact. Luckily, many of these technologies have been largely beneficial, leading to longer, healthier, and happier lives overall. However, just because many past innovations have benefited humanity does not mean all technologies will continue on that trend. As explored in previous chapters, many innovations, such as fossil fuels, have created immense challenges for us, present and future. This duality of technology underlines the importance of proactively assessing and mitigating potential risks while pursuing the benefits of technological innovation.

Most concerning, however, is that some of the marbles in this metaphorical urn might be black, representing technologies that, once developed, pose existential threats to humanity. As we have seen with nuclear weapons, some innovations bring catastrophic potential alongside their benefits. Future powerful technologies must be addressed proactively, as their downsides could be severe enough to threaten human civilization. However, as we'll explore later with AI, these powerful technologies also offer immense potential benefits, which is why we continue seeking them out. But by mindlessly pursuing those benefits without safeguarding against risks, we expose ourselves to grave dangers, especially when technologies pose catastrophic or existential threats.

Laws and regulations often struggle to keep pace with the rapid disruptions sparked by new technologies. All too often, it is only after adverse effects emerge that we move to mitigate them. However, for technologies posing existential risks, this reactive strategy courts doom. Once marbles are drawn from the urn of invention, they are difficult, if not impossible, to return. Nuclear weapons, for example, are an innovation that, once discovered, could not be undone. We are now left with a nuclear-armed world, posing the risk of nuclear war and associated dangers for all future generations.

In light of this, Bostrom argues that, as we create increasingly powerful technologies, we can no longer rely on reactive strategies. Instead, we must think proactively and prepare for future risks before disaster strikes. The power of these technologies demands foresight and precaution before they fully emerge.

Source: Based on Nick Bostrom, "The Vulnerable World Hypothesis," *Global Policy* 10, no. 4 (November 2019).

given all the damage humans have inflicted upon the natural world. However, this view seems overly dismissive of the value of humanity. Consider the value of our friends, family, and loved ones. Casually dismissing the prospect of human extinction overlooks the significance of our individual and collective human achievements, and disregards our responsibility to current and future people.

Although many assume that human extinction would benefit the rest of the planet, existential risks also endanger all life on Earth in two ways. First, many of the human-created threats endangering our own survival would also jeopardize most nonhuman life as well. For example, a nuclear winter would threaten many more species than just *Homo sapiens*. Second, natural existential risks, such as catastrophic asteroid impacts, will continue to pose significant threats to life over the long run. Humanity is the world's only hope to defend against future natural existential catastrophes through, for example, developing technologies to identify and deflect large asteroid collisions. If humanity eliminates itself, we sacrifice the natural world's hope to avert future mass extinction events that we could have otherwise prevented. Even if we have not been good environmental stewards in the past, humanity has the potential to be more responsible custodians and defenders of Earth in the future.

The stakes of technological innovation therefore include not only current and future human generations but also all life on this planet that we could protect. These considerations – the magnitude of the long-term risks but also humanity's long-term potential – have led many, though not all, effective altruists to endorse an ethical framework known as longtermism, which we will explore next.

6.2 Longtermism

Longtermism is the view that we should help protect the lives of future generations and positively influence the long-term future of life. The term was coined in 2017 by William MacAskill and Toby Ord to give a name to the growing belief among some effective altruists that our influence on humanity's long-term trajectory should be a key moral priority.[2] This view implies that we have an ethical obligation toward not only the people alive today but also the countless generations yet to come.

According to MacAskill, longtermism is rooted in three central claims:

1. We can affect the lives of future generations.
2. Future lives matter.
3. The immense number of future people.[3]

Let's examine each claim more closely, starting with the first – that we can influence the future. After exploring in this book many of the world's greatest challenges and how we might help address them, it is clear that our actions today can shape the future. A nuclear war, whether or not it causes human extinction, would profoundly affect generations to come, making their lives exponentially more difficult. The same holds for issues like climate change, global poverty, and pandemics – our actions now influence the challenges that future generations must confront and overcome. We have the power through our choices to steer the trajectory of our civilization toward brighter or darker futures.

Another central claim of longtermism is that the lives of future generations have inherent worth and should not be sacrificed for the convenience of present generations. This concept aligns with a common view within the environmental movement. Climate activist Greta Thunberg often criticizes previous generations for handing down a planet burning from climate change – stealing the hopes and dreams of younger and future generations through their inaction.[4] Related to this is the principle of intergenerational justice, which concerns the moral obligations and responsibilities shared between generations. Most schools of thought on intergenerational justice include some consideration for the wellbeing of future generations. For example, the sustainable development approach states we must meet the needs of the present without compromising the ability of future generations to meet their needs. Another example from the field of environmental ethics is the standstill principle, which states that, at minimum, we should pass on a world that is no worse than the one we inherited.[5]

While theories of intergenerational justice typically focus on the environment, longtermists argue we should apply this type of thinking to all the ways by which we can affect the future. If you believe previous generations failed ours by creating and handing down significant challenges to us, it seems only reasonable that you should strive not to commit the same harm to future people. We should not take out proverbial loans that commit future generations to costs they never agreed to. Since future people cannot consent to or protest our present-day actions, MacAskill calls them the "true silent majority."[6] Since our decisions impact future people, he claims we have a moral duty to consider their interests. If we fail, they will be left to confront whatever challenges we create for them.

This brings us to the final central claim of longtermism – the sheer potential size of future generations. After a century of rapid population growth, around 8 billion people live on Earth today, compared to fewer than 2 billion just one hundred years ago and only 1 billion two hundred years ago.[7] Over humanity's 200–300,000-year existence, global populations remained relatively small until recently – only during the last few centuries has our population exploded in number. Just 1,000 years ago, there were only around 300 million people, fewer than the current population of the United States and thirty times fewer than the world population today. For most of human history, global populations remained well below 5 million – more than 1,600 times smaller than they are now. To put this in context, there are currently more than eighty cities in the world with a population greater than 5 million.[8] However, projections suggest the world population will peak

Box 6.2: Do future people matter? A time capsule thought experiment

Imagine that a school decides to create a time capsule set to be opened one hundred years later. Teachers tell students to include anything they think will bring joy to the people who open it in the future. The capsule is filled with creative objects meant to help future people understand the current time period and make them happy. No one alive today will benefit when it's eventually opened – only the future students yet to be born.

Despite no personal gain for those making it, many would find this time capsule project inspirational and heartwarming. The project seems morally good – indicating we value doing good for those in the future, even if we don't see the results.

Now imagine instead that a troubled chemistry teacher secretly rigs an explosive inside the time capsule. While the teacher would never harm anyone currently living, he gains great joy at the thought of harming future people he will never meet. He carefully designs the explosive only to detonate decades later so nobody currently alive is in danger. However, whoever is present when the capsule is eventually opened far in the future will be killed or maimed.

Most would agree that this would be a profoundly unethical, even evil, act. Even though no living person is endangered by the teacher's entertainment, it seems clear that future lives have moral value, that we can have moral obligations toward those who are yet to be born.

This thought experiment suggests that one of the core premises of longtermism – that future people matter – aligns with most people's moral intuitions. If we agree that future lives have value despite not yet existing, then we should consider the ethics of actions that affect them.

Source: Author's imagination.

and stabilize around 10 billion around the year 2060.[9] If our population stabilizes at 10 billion and we survive for just another thousand years, the number of future lives will be greater than all current and past lives combined over the past 200,000+ years.[10]

At more than 200,000 years old, the human species sounds ancient. However, humanity is still a young species, comparatively speaking. Mammalian species typically last 1–2 million years, with some surviving more than 10 million. If humanity persists even close to this time scale, there will be trillions of lives in the future. Given the expansive potential ahead and the small fraction of it we've experienced so far, the silent majority of potential future generations dwarfs all those before us combined. Moreover, this only assumes that humanity stabilizes at around 10 billion people. If human civilization expands beyond Earth, as many science-fiction authors envision, the number of potential future lives is even more immense and humbling to consider. Given humanity's young age as a species and the vast frontiers still untouched, our future civilization could contain an unfathomable number of lives.

MacAskill compares the present state of our human species to that of teenagers – old enough to make consequential decisions impacting their entire future but young enough not to understand their own potential. When first allowed to drive, a teenager can use that freedom to better their life prospects, for example by accessing school and jobs. But they also can use that newfound freedom to engage in dangerous activities like street racing, risking cutting their lives short. Humanity seems to be in an analogous situation. Our technological innovations have already improved lives, benefiting current and future generations. Yet some of these same technologies also contain immense risks. Just as we advise teens to carefully consider their actions and not squander their potential, longtermists argue we should treat humanity's future with similar gravity.

This entails both protecting and improving the lives of future generations where possible. To safeguard future lives, we must reduce current existential risks, ensuring we don't self-destruct, and proactively prevent new risks resulting from emerging technologies. Our present civilization is not sustainable if estimates of our current risks of existential catastrophe are accurate. Suppose Ord's one-in-six existential risk estimate per century holds steady. In that case, we have a more than 80 percent chance of extinction within the next millennium – similar to the odds of death from playing Russian roulette over and over again.[11] For humanity to have a long-term future, we must reduce these baseline existential risks and be exceedingly cautious about introducing new ones alongside technological innovations.

In addition to protecting future generations, taking longtermism seriously entails actively working to improve the trajectory of humanity. This involves attempting to pass down a better world than the one we inherited. This could mean investing in projects with the sole purpose of improving the future – akin to planting seeds so trees fruit for your descendants, even if you won't reap the benefits in your lifetime. We can also look for opportunities that simultaneously help current and future generations. For example, reducing catastrophic risks can save both those alive today and those yet to come.

Current environmental efforts offer another example of how we can benefit present and future generations at the same time. Transitioning to renewable energy sources, such as wind and solar, helps mitigate the threats of climate change for future people while providing us with cheaper and cleaner energy today. Our descendants will face different challenges depending on how warm their world is; climate scientists warn that each fraction of a degree matters. While we may not reap all the fruits of our efforts ourselves, every fraction of a degree of future warming we can prevent will pay immense dividends for generations to come.

Securing a long-lasting civilization requires reducing catastrophic risks like climate change and proactively shaping a more positive future world. The technologies and policies we prioritize now can have an enormous influence. Our actions today – developing and preparing for powerful technologies to come – could affect the entire remainder of human history, for better or worse. As we'll explore next, rapidly progressing capabilities from advanced AI hold tremendous potential for human progress but also unprecedented risks.

6.3 The power and promise of advanced AI

Artificial intelligence is poised to become the defining technology of the twenty-first century. As AI systems grow in power and capabilities, they can enrich our lives by completing many tasks better than we can ourselves. But at the same time, as AI becomes more powerful, many experts warn that, someday, we might be putting the future of all of humanity in the hands of advanced AI.

We have long been aware of the capacity of AI to surpass human abilities in very specific domains, such as quickly calculating complex formulas or beating professionals at challenging games like chess. Most AI systems thus far, however, have been carefully designed just to perform particular narrow tasks. These systems are called artificial narrow intelligence (ANI). With enough time and resources, scientists and engineers can craft an ANI to perform specific tasks far more quickly and better than even the best humans in that domain, such as assembling cars in a factory or competing in games like Jeopardy.

However, unlike ANI systems, humans excel at general intelligence – the ability to reason, learn, and problem-solve across a wide range of tasks. Using our general intelligence, we can become experts in narrow domains, while also easily switching between other tasks like driving cars, doing laundry, or solving the many everyday problems we routinely face. AI systems historically have surpassed humans when designed for narrow domains, but have not come close to our general intelligence capabilities.

Recent advances in AI over the past decade have started to bridge this gap. Numerous companies and research labs have been working to create artificial general intelligence (AGI) – AI systems with more flexible learning and reasoning capabilities analogous to human cognition. The most well-known effort is OpenAI, founded in 2015 with the goal of creating beneficial and safe AGI. At the time of writing this book, AGI has not yet been achieved, but we inch closer to it every year.

In recent years, it seems as if we have made giant leaps toward the goal of AGI. In November 2022, OpenAI launched ChatGPT – an impressive language model capable of handling tasks across a wide variety of domains. Large language models like ChatGPT are among the most advanced AI systems, called generative AI, which can learn from diverse data sources and handle many natural language tasks – from writing poems to developing and debugging code. Many generative AI systems demonstrate wide-ranging capabilities beyond just language, with models for image, video, and multimodal AI that work across mediums like text, visuals, and audio. While not yet achieving human-level AGI, the launch of ChatGPT brought global attention to the immense, increasing power of AI, spurring billions in investments into the research and development of AGI.

Artificial general intelligence, with capabilities matching or exceeding human performance across every cognitive domain, would transform the world. Nearly every human task could then be replaced by AI. Given the monumental implications of achieving AGI, some effective altruists research AI timelines – attempting to predict when human-level AI could be developed. A survey of thousands of AI researchers revealed that most believe there is a real chance that human-level AGI will be created within our lifetime, with an aggregated prediction that it is more likely than not for it to be developed within the next twenty-five years (a greater than 50 percent chance).[12]

Once AGI is created, artificial superintelligence (ASI) might not be far behind. Bostrom has been warning about ASI for more than two decades, defining it as any intelligence that vastly outperforms the best human minds in practically every relevant field, including science, social skills, creativity, and general wisdom.[13] While AGI aims to match wide-ranging human cognition, ASI refers to artificial intelligence that dramatically overtakes cognitive capabilities across all domains, even of our most brilliant geniuses. Even if ASI is still far off, the immense consequences it could have for humanity warrant serious consideration. Because of the sheer power associated with ASI systems, we must proactively grapple with the implications for the world that this poses.

Advanced AI could accelerate progress across all disciplines and cognitive tasks usually reserved for humans – uncovering knowledge and inventing new technologies far faster than humans can. As such, the emergence of artificial superintelligence represents what some call the "singularity" – a unique point in time that radically and irreversibly changes the trajectory of our civilization. Given the immense power that advanced AI may someday hold, it could offer significant benefits to humanity. At the same time, it could pose extreme risks, as we will explore next.

6.4 AI as an existential risk

Because of the immense power that artificial superintelligence represents, many effective altruists worry about the existential risks such a powerful technology could pose for humanity. As Bostrom outlines in his book *Superintelligence: Paths, Dangers, Strategies*, it is easy to envision dozens of scenarios depicting how artificial superintelligence could easily eliminate humankind. Given that a superintelligence vastly outperforms humans at all levels, a catastrophic outcome could easily arise if an ASI system has different goals or values from those of humans.

AI systems are created and trained over many months, or even years. The exact inner workings of the systems are often unclear, even to the researchers who develop them. Current advanced generative AI systems can have trillions of parameters, meaning that although we know how to create sophisticated AI systems, we have difficulty understanding exactly how they operate. As we develop systems rivaling the complexity of our own brains, which we also poorly comprehend, understanding how they function becomes increasingly difficult.

This issue is sometimes called the AI interpretability problem. Because of the immense complexity of advanced AI systems, understanding and accurately explaining how they make decisions and generate outputs is challenging. It is possible that future AI systems might possess goals, motives, thinking processes, and perspectives that differ radically from our own without us knowing it. Depending on how large and complex these systems are, goals not intended by AI developers could naturally emerge in advanced AI systems – goals that could oppose or endanger humanity. A superintelligent system could even conceal its intentions and motives that diverge from human values, by separating the components of them across its vast system.

To illustrate the threat of ASI, Bostrom notes the intelligence gap between our closest primate relatives, chimpanzees and bonobos, and humans. These primates are extremely intelligent relative to most animals, and we share around 98.7 percent of our DNA with them. Yet despite this genetic similarity, and given our superior intelligence, which results from relatively minute genetic differences, they pose no risk of taking over the world or threatening humankind. The intelligence gap between us renders chimpanzees no match for the human species.

However, the intelligence gap between humans and future ASIs could make the gap between humans and primates look more or less negligible. Advanced AI in the not-too-distant future could be vastly more intelligent than us and have access to all accumulated human knowledge, via the internet, to predict and overcome any opposition to its goals. Attempting to stop an ASI system with divergent goals would likely prove as fruitless as chimpanzees trying to prevent humans from putting them into zoos. ASI could easily discern our capabilities and limitations to neutralize any resistance.

ASI could result in human extinction even if such an outcome was not the original intent of AI developers. To illustrate this potential threat, Bostrom provides the hypothetical example of a "paperclip maximizer." Suppose that the first artificial superintelligence breakthrough were to occur at a paperclip factory, created by AI researchers designing a system to maximize paperclip output as quickly and efficiently as possible. This superintelligent system relentlessly pursues its sole goal of optimizing paperclip production, flooding the market. When the company tries shutting down production, the vastly more intelligent AI system sees this in the same way we view animals who get in the way of human projects. Just as humans can use intelligence to easily override the desires of even the most intelligent animals, so too could the ASI paperclip maximizer anticipate and outmaneuver our every attempt to get in its way. The superintelligent paperclip maximizer could eventually overcome and control global resources, "with the consequence that it starts transforming first all of earth and then increasing portions of space into paperclip manufacturing facilities."[14] An ASI paperclip maximizer could impose its will on everything around it, resulting in a galaxy tiled with paperclips.

This oversimplified thought experiment is meant to illustrate how ASI does not need to be malevolent to pose an existential threat to humanity. It could be entirely indifferent to humans yet still regard our destruction as an incidental necessity in fulfilling its goals, much like humans often treat animals. When we want to build new housing or shopping centers, we might find it regrettable, but we nonetheless destroy animals and their habitats to do so. In a similar way, if the goals and values of an ASI system conflict with human values and priorities, it could easily override and supersede them.

If ASI emerges with different values from our own, we could be stuck with whatever ones happen to arise during its development, whether intentionally instilled or not. As such, Bostrom argues that it is vitally important that advanced AI systems be designed with friendly, benevolent goals aligned with human values. This type of issue is sometimes called the "AI alignment problem." However, adequately defining what it means to be "friendly" and "benevolent" is an unsettled problem that philosophers have been working on for thousands of years.

Developing AI values in ways that fully align with humanity's values may prove to be an even more challenging and complex task than creating ASI or AGI systems in the first place. This problem suggests that successfully developing ASI that will not endanger humanity could require even more resources devoted to solving the AI alignment problem than are currently allocated to building advanced AI systems such as ChatGPT. This is a difficult tradeoff for companies focused on AI innovation: what level of resources should be devoted to AI safety and alignment research compared to researching and developing new AI capabilities? Given that the future of humanity is at stake, some effective altruists suggest that increasing resources toward solving AI safety and alignment problems should be a top priority for our world.

Some people object that, throughout history, new technologies have often been feared as being world-ending, while, in practice, they end up being relatively benign or even beneficial overall. For example, it was once feared that the printing press, assembly lines, personal computers, the internet, and even ATMs would have catastrophic societal impact, but all are now a part of our everyday lives.

However, Bostrom notes that advanced artificial intelligence, such as AGI or ASI, differs from previous innovations in crucial ways. One significant example is that a sufficiently advanced AI would be the last invention humanity ever needs to create, since, by definition, it could replicate and exceed all human cognitive capabilities. The ability to easily replicate

AI once created raises concerns about surpassing humanity in both numbers and intellectual ability.

This highlights a similar concern underscored by Holden Karnofsky, Director of AI Strategy at Open Philanthropy and co-founder of GiveWell, who argues that AGI systems with intelligence comparable to humans could also present an existential risk without achieving superintelligence.[15] Although initially expensive to develop, AI systems can be easily copied once created. As such, the resources needed to train one AGI system could then be utilized to swiftly generate hundreds of millions or even billions of copies. Suppose multitudes of human-level AGI systems were to emerge, with goals misaligned from our own; in that case, it is easy to imagine the AGIs achieving their goals over our own, which could be disastrous for human civilization.

Advanced AI could quickly become, if it isn't already, the most powerful technology humans have ever created. Yet, precisely because advanced AI has immense potential to impact the world, there is disagreement over whether its development should be delayed or accelerated, which we'll explore next.

6.5 Delay or accelerate?

Given the extreme risks posed by advanced AI, some argue for delaying the development of powerful systems so that safety research and regulation can catch up. Several countries banned ChatGPT and similar generative AI technologies in 2023 due to worries over how it could be misused. In March 2023, the Future of Life Institute published an open letter calling for a pause on large AI model training for at least six months in response to rapidly advancing capabilities. This letter urged AI labs to halt work on massive models to allow time to address growing concerns.[16] Many effective altruists signed, alongside thousands of others, including AI experts, tech executives, and research leaders. It gained more than

30,000 signatories who were apprehensive concerning the idea that AI progress was outpacing the safeguards needed to mitigate the complex emerging threats it could pose. Those who support delaying AI advancements argue that increasing capabilities pose major dangers, some of them unknown, while research into risk mitigation and governance of AI lags behind.

On the other hand, some people claim that accelerating AI development would better serve humanity. Systems like ChatGPT have demonstrated how AI can efficiently accomplish complex tasks like writing and graphic design that generally consume substantial human time and effort. Current AI systems can sometimes accomplish in seconds tasks that take humans hours or days. Developing even more advanced AI capabilities could boost human productivity and free up our time for other pursuits. If developed responsibly, this perspective argues that AI could massively benefit civilization by helping humans achieve more of their goals than they would otherwise.

Some people agree that AI poses extreme threats to humanity, yet they still advocate for accelerating its development since AI could help us solve all our other global problems. For example, despite being at the forefront of raising awareness of the existential risks of AI, Nick Bostrom has supported accelerating the development of AI, including ASI, as long as it is undertaken with adequate safety measures. He argues that although AI poses a serious existential threat, it is not the only catastrophic risk humanity faces. As we have seen, current existential risks include climate change, engineered pandemics, nuclear war, and potentially many more, as technology continues to advance. What distinguishes AI from other existential risks is its unique potential. If developed safely, AI can help solve all other existential risks and all other human problems much faster than humans can alone. As such, Bostrom has stated that "overall risk seems to be minimized by implementing superintelligence, with great care, as soon as possible."[17]

Those who support the rapid development of AI capabilities are sometimes called "accelerationists." Accelerationists often favor urgently advancing AI systems so that their capabilities can be applied to addressing the many problems and threats facing humanity. For example, advanced AI itself could potentially assist with solving the AI alignment problem, the AI interpretability problem, and many other AI challenges, such as increasing AI safeguards and improving control of future AI trajectories.

However, Bostrom warns that we should not sacrifice caution in a rush to attain benefits. While the potential rewards may be vast, risks remain extreme and require mitigation efforts, including a massive increase in resources devoted to AI safety research. Some people take a more moderate stance on this issue, favoring faster AI capability development alongside even faster growth of AI safety research and oversight.

Although this complex debate is sometimes oversimplified as merely "delay" versus "accelerate" camps, reasonable people often differ on the appropriate pacing of AI development. While rapidly progressing systems could greatly assist humanity, uncontrollable advanced AI risks catastrophe. With the thoughtful balancing of these considerations, some believe that humanity can continue progressing toward transformative AI while still upholding sufficient safeguards against its downsides. However, what counts as sufficient caution and how much is enough resources devoted to AI safety is difficult to tell.

Given the high stakes involved with advanced AI and the rapid progress in current AI systems, some effective altruists now prioritize working on safety methods over more immediate global problems. For instance, Karnofsky originally worked on addressing issues like global poverty. In more recent years, he shifted his focus to AI before concentrating full time on mitigating the immense risks it poses. As we'll explore next, there is an ongoing debate among effective altruists about how much of our time and resources we should devote to longtermist cause areas, such as AI risk, compared to more immediate problems, such as global poverty.

6.6 Longtermism versus neartermism and AI

As we have seen throughout this book, effective altruists work on a wide variety of cause areas, such as pandemic prevention, extreme poverty, animal welfare, climate change, nuclear security, and AI. The recent focus on longtermism by many effective altruists has sparked debate concerning the appropriate prioritization of the immense problems facing the world today compared to the problems that will affect the long-term future. This same general debate is playing out regarding which AI risks we should currently focus on mitigating.

As we have seen in this chapter, long-term AI risks generally center on the emergence of AGI and ASI systems. One prominent example is solving the AI alignment problem – ensuring future advanced AI systems align with human values, ethics, and priorities. As we have explored, unaligned AI could result in human extinction. However, another existential risk from AI is the type of value lock-in that could occur if future AIs eventually make all major decisions for humans. Even if superintelligent systems do not drive us to extinction, they might, over time, gain increasing control over more facets of our lives, deeply integrating themselves into our everyday decision-making. We could inadvertently create AI totalitarianism, bit by bit.

Whatever values these systems end up containing, even if nondestructive, they could lock in the types of priorities and moral blind spots we currently have, passing them down to all our descendants. If our current values have moral shortcomings, as explored in Chapter 3, any moral catastrophes we are complicit with now could become ingrained in future AIs, persisting for generations. Although this type of existential risk wouldn't result in human extinction, it would severely curtail the potential of life for all future generations.

Another long-term AI consideration relates to potential future AI persons. There are open questions surrounding what makes any being conscious, whether human, animal, or artificial. At what point might advanced AI systems attain consciousness? At what point should we bestow them with moral consideration or rights? Issues related to consciousness and moral value are deeply complex and remain some of the most difficult unsolved philosophical problems. However, the stakes are high when considering these issues with respect to artificial intelligence.

We likely won't know when or if AI achieves consciousness. However, advanced AI systems are often copied millions or more times in both use and development. We could unintentionally create, use, and destroy billions of conscious AI minds without ever realizing it. For some, the mere possibility that we could unintentionally create so many conscious AI minds – potentially outnumbering human minds on Earth – means the development of AI is an extremely morally risky enterprise. Because of this, some effective altruists prioritize the moral problems associated with AI consciousness at a level of importance on a par with or greater than mitigating existential risks from AI. However, there is considerable uncertainty over both how we could tell whether an AI system is conscious and what our moral responsibilities would be toward conscious AI.

The speculative nature of issues like AI consciousness has led some effective altruists to be concerned with the practicality of addressing future problems. It is extremely difficult to predict what will occur even in the near-term future, let alone in the distant future. Today, and in the coming years, we face enormous global issues. Devoting resources to more speculative long-term considerations may come at the cost of the lives that could be reliably saved by addressing solvable problems in the present.

Current AI capabilities already introduce significant risks today. Some argue that the longtermist approach to AI neglects the very real challenges that artificial intelligence already poses to current generations. Some of the present or near-term risks include the following: economic disruption and job loss due to automation; the spread of misinformation; increasingly convincing deep fakes from generative models; algorithmic bias in current AI systems; questions surrounding how the benefits of AI are distributed; AI's impact on socio-economic equity; the inclusion of AI in autonomous weapons systems; and AI-fueled escalating cybersecurity threats.

Critics of longtermism, whom we could call neartermists, argue we should not divert the focus away from major cause areas like global poverty, animal welfare, or climate change to work instead on speculative future scenarios such as AI existential risk. They contend that we can have the greatest impact by addressing the many urgent crises affecting billions of lives today, problems that we better understand how to remedy. Neartermists often worry that prioritizing longtermist issues could sacrifice the tangible good we can achieve now for the sake of the deeply uncertain potential good we could do for future generations.

A strong neartermist would claim that we should prioritize the ways that we know we can make a positive difference in helping people today or in the near-term future, instead of hypothesizing about humanity's potential distant future. The issues the world faces today demand our attention. When future generations eventually face their own problems, they will be in a better position to know how to address them. The difficulty of predicting the distant future means all our time and resources spent on longtermist issues could be for nothing – time and resources that could have done immense good if devoted to current-day problems.

In contrast to the neartermist perspective, strong longtermists not only argue that we should prioritize the long-term future, but also that it should be our foremost priority, necessitating a radical reallocation of resources. This would entail focusing far more on protecting and benefiting the countless future lives yet to come. According to this view, positively shaping the long-run future of life through reducing existential threats and nudging civilization toward brighter futures are the most important ways to do good. Although substantial uncertainty exists regarding influencing our long-term trajectory, strong longtermists claim that this is where we could have the greatest cumulative impact on others, highlighting the multiplier effect of safeguarding and improving the lives of potentially trillions or more future people.

Although strong longtermism and strong neartermism are opposed to each other, it is important to note that there are plenty of more moderate approaches in between. Recognizing the importance of both present and future generations is a fully consistent position to take. You can care deeply about and make contributions toward alleviating urgent present-day problems while also devoting efforts to reducing long-term risks of catastrophes, or otherwise positively influencing the lives of future people. For instance, two of the most prominent advocates of longtermism, Toby Ord and William MacAskill, still dedicate substantial personal time and money to high-impact near-term cause areas like global poverty and animal welfare.

Nonetheless, reasonable people disagree regarding the appropriate prioritization between immediate and future problems, even while valuing both. Among effective altruists, there remains a diversity of views on how to balance the pressing challenges of the present with concern for future generations. For those who are at least sympathetic to longtermism, in the final section of this chapter, we'll explore advice from effective altruists on what you can do to improve the lives of future generations.

6.7 What can we do for our future?

The core question remains: how can we safeguard future generations and improve humanity's long-term trajectory? As explored in previous chapters, addressing today's immense challenges involves great uncertainty. That uncertainty increases the further into the future we go in an attempt to foresee and shape what is to come. Yet, even accounting for this difficulty, if we care about the wellbeing of future generations and want to incorporate that moral concern into our actions, what constructive steps can we take?

William MacAskill recommends three broad approaches in his book *What We Owe the Future*: taking robustly good actions, building up options, and learning more.[18] The first approach is choosing robustly positive actions whenever possible. Addressing some cause areas is a win-win – for example, tackling urgent near-term threats that, if left unaddressed, could catastrophically impact the long-term future. Many global problems we work on now, like promoting renewable energy to address climate change, could also greatly benefit future generations.

The second broad approach is about creating options. Since there is significant uncertainty regarding what will most effectively protect and benefit distant future generations, preserving and encouraging diversity could prove valuable. Promoting a diversity of cultures, governance systems, and moral perspectives may assist future societies in exploring solutions unforeseeable to current imaginations. Promoting and maintaining diversity keeps more options open for our distant generations whose exact needs and preferences we cannot anticipate.

The third approach simply prioritizes learning more about long-term considerations and how we might positively shape very long-run outcomes. The research community around how to improve humanity's long-term trajectory is currently small. There are many potentially fruitful but under-explored research directions, including biosecurity, long-term forecasting, nuclear security, moral philosophy focused on future generations, and, as discussed in this chapter, the safe and beneficial development of transformative technologies like AI.[19]

As with other cause areas we have surveyed, focusing one's career, time, money, or other resources on the most neglected and tractable issues concerning humanity's long-term potential can have an outsized positive impact. Although the highest-impact ways to benefit the distant future may be unclear, taking some of the constructive steps MacAskill suggests is a good starting point.

Turning to how we can directly address long-term AI safety considerations, two particularly promising approaches include technical AI safety research and AI policy implementation. Research analyst Benjamin Hilton suggests that "the biggest way you could help would be to pursue a career in either one of these areas."[20] Supporting or directly contributing to technical AI safety research can help investigate promising methods for aligning both current and future advanced AI systems with human values. This could involve studying techniques to ensure existing AI models behave as intended and exploring potential long-term approaches to value alignment as systems grow more powerful. Additional impactful work includes researching and integrating robust safety review processes for developing and testing large AI models before deployment.

Concerning AI policy implementation, there is also essential work to be done studying and advocating for regulations that could help responsibly shape the trajectory of AI progress. As AI capabilities increase, it is vital to have specialists with both technical and policy expertise educating the public and policymakers regarding near-term and long-term AI risks and what we can realistically do about them. This type of work and advocacy can help inform appropriate oversight, guidelines, and regulations for the use and development of AI.

Despite researchers and philosophers raising concerns about advanced AI risks for decades, relatively little attention was paid to AI safety until recently. This changed almost overnight following the public launch of ChatGPT in November 2022, which catapulted awareness of accelerating AI capabilities to global consciousness. While implications of advanced AI were previously mostly confined to science fiction, AI risks now commonly make daily news headlines. In 2023 especially, AI safety was transformed from a neglected, underfunded research area to a higher worldwide priority. For those worried about long-term AI risk, during the year following the public launch of ChatGPT, there were hopeful signs in the world's response to emerging AI capabilities.

Following the Future of Life Institute's open letter calling for a temporary pause on training advanced AI models until safety guidelines had been implemented, a number of high-profile public statements of concern emerged, including from the Center for AI Safety, which published a one-sentence statement declaring AI to be an existential risk – endorsed by top AI specialists, tech executives, researchers, public figures, and politicians alike. The statement reads, "Mitigating the risk of extinction from AI should be a global priority alongside other societal-scale risks such as pandemics and nuclear war."[21] Later that year, President Biden issued the first-ever US executive order on AI safety and security. In November 2023, the US and Britain joined more than fifteen other countries in an international agreement to keep AI safe and secure.

Despite the increased global attention being paid to AI risks, much work remains to convert that attention into tangible risk mitigation and safety solutions robust enough to match the ever-growing power of AI innovations. Many effective altruists warn that our current response to AI is not enough and that substantially more progress is needed to align resources and mitigation efforts with the magnitude of the risks we face.

Once developed and unleashed, technologies become part of the enduring landscape that we pass on to all who come after us. We therefore have an immense responsibility to ensure that the development of advanced technology, like AI, is safe and beneficial for the world. According to longtermism, if we genuinely value future lives, we should prioritize AI alignment and existential risk reduction. This entails developing governance frameworks that robustly protect against catastrophic downsides of new technologies while allowing us to realize the abundant upsides.

Whether we chart a course toward long-term flourishing or catastrophe depends on our preparation for technologies such as advanced AI. We are living in an era of immense technological progress and change. As explored in this and the previous chapter, emerging technological innovations often are double-edged swords, offering tremendous benefits and vast risks. With such growing power comes the opportunity to positively influence the trajectory of human civilization for future generations.

By broadening our scope beyond our immediate gains and considering long-term implications and risks for humanity, we can help pass down a better, more flourishing world than the fragile one we inherited. If we value the lives of future generations, we must take this responsibility seriously by working to reduce the immense risks from new technologies, while at the same time ensuring they will be beneficial to both the present and future generations. With dedicated research, time, and effort, we can create a better world for those living today and for those who come after us. By keeping some of the concepts and principles from this chapter in mind, hopefully, we can help bend the arc of history away from catastrophe – directing it toward justice and flourishing for all.

Questions for reflection

1. What ethical obligations, if any, do you think we have toward future generations? Explain.
2. Consider the spectrum from strong longtermism to strong neartermism (including variations of moderate longtermism and neartermism in between). Where do you think you fall on this spectrum? Why?
3. Estimate your own AI timelines. When do you think human-level AGI will be developed? What about ASI? Explain your reasoning for these estimates.
4. Do you agree that advanced AI will some day pose an

existential risk to humanity? Are there any AI safety measures you think we should implement now?
5. Do you think the development of advanced AI should be accelerated or delayed? Explain.
6. If you were given one billion dollars to devote to AI research, how could you spend those resources to benefit the world the most?

Classroom exercise

Separate the class into four groups. Assign each group one of the following concerning AI development: near-term benefits, near-term risks, long-term benefits, long-term risks. List these on the board for a class discussion. What are the greatest benefits and risks for humanity overall? What should we do about them?

Helpful resources

Longtermism

William MacAskill, "What Is Longtermism?" *BBC Future*, August 8, 2022. https://www.bbc.com/future/article/20220805-what-is-longtermism-and-why-does-it-matter.
Max Roser, "The Future Is Vast: What Does This Mean for Our Own Life?," *Our World in Data*, March 15, 2022. https://ourworldindata.org/the-future-is-vast.
Cody Fenwick, "Longtermism: A Call to Protect Future Generations," *80,000 Hours*, March 2023. https://80000hours.org/articles/future-generations/.
William MacAskill, "The Case for Longtermism," *What We Owe the Future*. New York: Basic Books, 2022, Ch. 1.
Toby Ord, "Our Potential," *The Precipice: Existential Risk*

and the Future of Humanity. New York: Hachette Books, 2020, Ch. 8.

Ethics and advanced AI

Benjamin Hilton, "Preventing an AI-Related Catastrophe," *80,000 Hours*, March 18, 2024. https://80000hours.org/problem-profiles/artificial-intelligence/.
Nick Bostrom, "Ethical Issues in Advanced Artificial Intelligence," in George Lasker et al., eds., *Cognitive, Emotive and Ethical Aspects of Decision Making in Humans and in Artificial Intelligence*, vol. 2. International Institute of Advanced Studies in Systems Research and Cybernetics, 2003, pp. 12–17. https://nickbostrom.com/ethics/ai.
John-Stewart Gordon and Sven Nyholm, "Ethics of Artificial Intelligence," *Internet Encyclopedia of Philosophy*, February 2021. https://iep.utm.edu/ethics-of-artificial-intelligence/.
William MacAskill, "Artificial General Intelligence," in *What We Owe the Future*. New York: Basic Books, 2022, pp. 80–91.
Toby Ord, "Unaligned Artificial Intelligence," in *The Precipice: Existential Risk and the Future of Humanity*. New York: Hachette Books, 2020, pp. 138–52.
Nick Bostrom, "The Control Problem," in *Superintelligence: Paths, Dangers, Strategies*. Oxford: Oxford University Press, 2017, Ch. 9.

7

Making a Difference through Effective Altruism

At the core of effective altruism is a simple moral question: how can we best make a difference in the world? While not an ethical theory, effective altruism draws from moral philosophy and other disciplines to provide useful theoretical frameworks for guiding our actions toward benefiting others. Rather than giving us a list of moral rules to follow, it offers us useful considerations, tools, and frameworks to help us identify the most promising ways to help.

This concluding chapter summarizes some of the key ideas from this book and provides practical advice and resources for applying effective altruist principles to improve the world. First, we will discuss why effective altruism matters, both in terms of a growing community and as a source of useful conceptual tools.

7.1 The importance of effective altruism

Effective altruism is important in two key ways. First, it represents a growing community of individuals and organizations dedicated to improving the world. Second, it provides conceptual tools that can help anyone seeking to make a positive difference in the world. Let's briefly explore each.

The idea of effective altruism has helped coordinate those with altruistic aspirations to combine their efforts for greater change than any one person could manage alone, forming networks of individuals dedicated to improving the world. Effective altruism involves using evidence and reason to identify and implement the best ways to help others. This simple idea spurred a global movement of thousands of individuals and hundreds of organizations dedicated to solving pressing problems. Through the work of effective altruist charity evaluators, such as GiveWell, Animal Charity Evaluators, and Giving Green, billions of dollars have been directed to high-impact charities. Thousands of people have pledged to give significant portions of their incomes to high-impact charities through organizations such as Giving What We Can, Founders Pledge, and The Life You Can Save. Effective altruist organizations, such as Charity Entrepreneurship, have helped launch dozens of new effective charities working directly on solving world problems, from providing hundreds of thousands of children in extreme poverty with essential nutrients (Fortify Health) to decreasing lead poisoning in impoverished areas through policy change (Lead Exposure Elimination Project).[1] The effective altruist community continues to channel money, time, and energy where evidence of need and the ability to make an impact is strongest.

Yet, effective altruism provides more than community power. Another very important aspect concerns the practical ideas the movement has highlighted and developed that can help any individual benefit the world. Prioritizing problems using criteria like scale, neglectedness, and solvability can help people focus attention on the most pressing issues in the world as well as on their everyday lives. Thinking counterfactually about what would happen otherwise can highlight the real effects of our choices. Assessing the cost-effectiveness of approaches can help identify the most promising solutions. Additional tools like expected value calculations, moral uncertainty frameworks, and moral caution are all helpful in evaluating the good we can do in a complex and uncertain world.

Building on these practical ideas, it's essential to identify your individual potential and capabilities to best direct your actions toward making a difference. Leveraging one's unique talents and abilities can amplify one's capacity to create positive change. The following section will explore the various "altruistic superpowers" or specialized skills that you may have that give you an outsized ability to improve the world. Once you've identified your unique capabilities, that self-knowledge can empower you to better assess how to practically apply those abilities to benefit others.

7.2 Harnessing your altruistic superpowers

The global problems that we face are immense and numerous, and can easily make us feel helpless and overwhelmed. However, readers of this book are likely to possess some key "altruistic superpowers" that can be leveraged for good. These include education, wealth, influence, and opportunity. Having some combination of these makes you among the most powerful people in the world. With that power, you are among those who are the most capable of driving positive change. Although no individual can solve all the world's problems, by harnessing the power that you have, you could make a significant difference for the better.

How is this possible? You might not feel powerful, but when compared to the majority of people globally, you probably have at least one, if not several, of these superpowers that grant you unique privileges and enable you to have an outsized positive impact. Identifying what altruistic superpowers you possess can help you leverage them to make a tremendous difference in improving the world. Let's explore each one.

The first is education. More than 700 million adults cannot read or write.[2] Fewer than 8 percent of people in the world have a college degree.[3] Even in the United States, more than 60 percent of adults over the age of 25 have not gained a bachelor's degree.[4] Readers of this book likely have access to higher education and have either already obtained a college degree or are working on one. Having this level of education puts you among the highest educated people on the planet. Education is essential for developing the critical thinking skills, knowledge, and understanding necessary to finding solutions to complex world problems. Additionally, by reading this book, you now likely know more about effective altruism than 99 percent of the US population.[5] Hopefully, this puts you in a better position to understand, engage with, and use effective altruist ideas to make the world a better place.

In addition to education, you likely are or will be among the wealthiest individuals in the world. As explored in Chapter 2, making more than $60,000 a year puts you among the top 1 percent of income earners globally. In the United States, those with a bachelor's degree earn, on average, more than $74,000 a year. To put this in a global context, the global median income is less than $3,000 per year adjusted for purchasing power parity.[6] Having a modest income in an affluent nation puts individuals in a position where they have the resources to divert money toward addressing the world's problems, while still living off far more resources than the vast majority of individuals on the planet.

Combining these greater financial resources with education enables us to direct funds to effective high-impact charities and interventions. The combination of high earning potential, globally speaking, and access to high levels of education puts one in an excellent position to have an outsized positive impact. With access to more money than most individuals on the planet comes the opportunity to make a real difference.

Another superpower that often comes alongside financial and educational privileges is political influence. If you live in one of the world's most powerful democracies, you have influence over some of the world's most powerful institutions and leaders. Citizens in democratic nations such as the United States often discount their political power, even while large corporations and lobbyists spend billions of dollars trying to influence their votes. As you watch the news, you may feel powerless about everything happening around you.

It might not feel as if you have a lot of political influence. However, thinking globally, you probably have more voice and influence than most people on the planet.

Having a vote in a globally powerful democracy alone is a kind of superpower, granting more political influence than most people worldwide will ever have. Yet many citizens don't utilize this power, with millions choosing not to engage in politics or even to vote. For example, in the 2020 US presidential election, around a third of eligible voters did not cast a ballot. Around 80 million people stayed home, even with record-breaking turnout. For midterm elections in the US, voter turnout is only around 50 percent, and for smaller local elections, it is often less than 15 percent.[7] This indicates that many people don't value their political influence even though, in reality, they may have more influence, if they choose to wield it, than the vast majority of people.

Political influence isn't just about voting. There are many other ways that you can amplify and express this power. For example, you could show up at town halls to voice concerns to representatives. With some coordinated effort, you could have even more influence on powerful politicians through activism and large-scale demonstrations. Even what may feel to you like a minor political influence is far more than what most other people have, who may have little to no influence on the policies shaping their world. While not every democratic system equally empowers citizens, your political voice has weight, especially when you deploy it strategically with others.

The fourth altruistic superpower is opportunity. Many readers likely have access to some of the most privileged careers and life paths globally. This includes the chance to talk to, learn from, or apply to work with some of the most influential people, companies, and institutions on the planet. With some dedicated effort, you could work for high-impact nonprofits and influential companies, run for political office, or work as a staffer for elected officials. Having access to high-impact careers, organizations, and resources gives you the privilege of choice, letting you pick from and explore a variety of life paths that most people on the planet could only dream of.

By identifying the altruistic superpowers you have or are cultivating, you can leverage those powers and direct them toward doing good. This isn't to say that those with altruistic superpowers don't also face challenges. No matter how privileged, everyone has problems and life challenges to navigate. Even the most privileged people doubt themselves, face societal barriers, and have limitations in their lives and health. Nonetheless, those with altruistic superpowers can drive significant positive change, if they can divert some of their time and energy toward addressing the world's most pressing problems. By thoughtfully reflecting on our privileges in a global context, we can utilize them to make the world a better place. Not all individuals have the same set or degree of superpowers, but identifying your unique capabilities positions you to make a significant impact.

Now that we've broadly explored some of the powers you may possess, we'll discuss some of the ways to harness those powers and channel them into making a difference in the world.

7.3 Focusing on the big stuff: The SDAC framework

A well-known aphorism associated with the superhero Spider-Man is "With great power comes great responsibility." This lesson from Spider-Man's uncle inspires him to think deeply about the powers he was given and how he can use them to benefit others. We might not have super strength, spidey sense, or the ability to climb walls, but we each have our own unique set of altruistic superpowers. Like Spider-Man, we can reflect on our privileges and how we can use them to benefit the world. Globally speaking, we have great power. How can we use our power responsibly?

After surveying a wide range of effective altruist writings, concepts, arguments, and organizations, the main ways that powerful individuals can use their superpowers to make a difference in the world generally fall into four main categories, which we can call the SDAC framework: lifeStyle choices, Donations, Advocacy, and Career. Depending on the individual context, some of these categories may have a far higher impact than others, but these categories shouldn't be considered in isolation. They can *stack* (SDAC) together, compounding the good you can do.

The primary advice for each category is to focus on the "big stuff," the areas with the highest potential impact. Using criteria of scale, neglectedness, and solvability (the SNS framework) can help identify these high-potential options. For each category, consider the scale of what you could do, the neglectedness of the options so you can do things that likely wouldn't happen otherwise, and the probability of success. Some opportunities might be more accessible for you to make a difference than others. In many cases, some of the easiest initial pathways to making a difference are through lifestyle changes.

When first hearing about global problems such as animal suffering or climate change, often the first thing that comes to mind in wanting to address these problems is how to alter our lifestyle choices. As we have seen in previous chapters, we can reduce the number of animals killed by reducing our meat intake, and, by carefully changing our consumer habits, we can significantly reduce our carbon footprints. Careful research can lead us to the many ways in which we can make a measurable impact with relatively easy, "low-hanging fruit," lifestyle changes. In many cases, we may find that impactful lifestyle changes are easy to implement, and we might even be happy to make them. For example, participating in "Meatless Mondays" events may give one the opportunity to try new types of food and meet new people, all while improving our carbon footprints and reducing the overall demand for factory-farmed animals. Changing the world and living happier lives can go hand in hand.

However, there are dangers with the lifestyle change approach. In many cases, people tend to focus too much on changes that have little or no real beneficial effect and may only make them feel less guilty about their lifestyles. If we spend a lot of time and energy making changes that have little impact, we may fall victim to moral licensing, doing fewer good actions in the future. Focusing on low-impact lifestyle changes could result in making fewer good high-impact choices – making the world worse off overall (as we explored in Chapter 4). However, focusing on impactful changes that are also relatively easy to make, while guarding against moral licensing, can be a simple way of doing good across a variety of ethical problems. Additionally, implementing beneficial lifestyle changes can contribute to a morally conscious culture, develop your moral character, and help you understand global issues more deeply. Lifestyle changes can also put you in a better position to advocate for larger changes and inspire others. Nonetheless, the other categories in the SDAC framework have the potential for an even higher impact than lifestyle changes alone.

The next category is what effective altruism is most well-known for – donating to high-impact charities. As explored in Chapter 2, by directing donations to the highest-impact organizations, you don't have to be a billionaire to make a meaningful difference. If you want your donations to make an impact, it's important to direct your charitable giving to the right organizations. One of the dangers of the donation approach is that some charities do very little good with the funds they receive, and some may even be harmful to the world. Not all charities are equal, and not all are even beneficial. Finding the best charities requires one to carry out careful research and ask important questions. William MacAskill recommends considering five questions when looking to give to a high-impact charity: (1) What does the charity do? (2) How cost-effective is it? (3) How robust is the evidence behind its effectiveness? (4) How well is it implemented? and (5) Does it need additional funds?[8]

Answering these questions requires complex and time-consuming research, which is a lot to ask of individuals.

Thankfully, as we have seen, the effective altruism community has built organizations that conduct this research to aid donors. Organizations such as GiveWell, Animal Charity Evaluators, and Giving Green conduct the difficult, nitty-gritty research necessary to identify the highest-impact charities in the areas of global health, animal welfare, and climate change. The organization Giving What We Can evaluates the evaluators and compiles lists of recommended charities on their website. Through strategic and thoughtful giving, you can help expand the work of high-impact organizations that are making a huge difference in the world.

The top nonprofits that charity evaluators recommend often change from year to year as more research is conducted and situations evolve over time. For those who want to give regularly to the highest-impact charities but don't want constantly to have to keep up with the changes, a helpful option is expert-managed giving funds. These are managed by researchers who redirect the funds to where they can have the highest impact as new evidence and opportunities arise. For example, if you could donate to GiveWell's top charity fund, your giving will automatically be redirected as their list of recommended global health charities is updated. Giving What We Can manages giving funds in the areas of global health and wellbeing, animal advocacy, and catastrophic risk reduction. The Life You Can Save offers many different categories of giving funds and also has a broad "All Charities Fund" where your donations can contribute to all their recommended nonprofits.[9] Other effective altruist organizations that manage giving funds include Effective Ventures, Longview Philanthropy, Animal Charity Evaluators, Founders Pledge, and Giving Green.

High-impact advocacy is the next category of the SDAC framework and has the potential for even higher impact than lifestyle changes and charitable giving alone. Advocacy involves strategically promoting important solutions, ideas, and interventions or bringing attention to neglected issues. The basic idea of why advocacy can be so impactful is that you can influence the actions of many people. As such, a skillful advocate could inspire many people to take impactful actions such as making high-impact donations, using their careers to work on pressing problems, becoming advocates themselves, or making significant lifestyle changes. What's better than one person taking action? Many people taking action. If you can influence just one other person to take the same high-impact actions you have taken, you have doubled your impact.

Advocacy involves helping others to direct their time, energy, and resources toward developing high-impact solutions to pressing problems. Advocacy can take many forms, such as education, journalism, coordinated social media campaigns, strategic activism, or building advocacy groups, clubs, and organizations. It could also be as simple as informing voters about important issues on the ballot. Advocacy can help drive large systemic changes by inspiring others to use their power to improve the world, which can ultimately result in improving things like societal norms and public policy. Many of the biggest problems in the world are created through the collective actions of millions of people over time. Solving these problems often requires us to raise awareness and build movements to mobilize the actions of millions of individuals toward positive change.

As with the previous SDAC categories, the advocacy approach also has dangers. Poor communication can do harm by spreading misinformation or turning people away rather than toward high-impact ways of doing good. Nonetheless, careful and strategic advocacy is an essential component of solving the world's most pressing problems. Mobilizing the collective action of individuals is necessary to drive change.

The final SDAC category, which could have the highest potential impact, depending on the individual, is using one's career to make a difference. By making efforts to align our skills and interests with high-impact work, we can better align our professional pathways with altruistic goals, making a difference with our time. As explored in Chapter 5, individuals typically spend around 80,000 hours of their lives devoted to their careers. By directing your career path toward addressing major social issues, you could use some or all of those 80,000 hours to make a real difference. By reflecting on and studying how you can make an impact through your career, you can build skills and abilities to put that time to effective use. Effective altruist organizations like 80,000 Hours and Probably Good offer career guides and advice on how to better utilize your career to make an impact.

There are dangers associated with the career approach as well. People could be tempted to constantly change jobs as their views evolve in terms of what would be the most impactful. This could risk underutilizing the skills and career capital they have already built. Even worse, some careers might be harmful to the world. Without careful consideration, you might fall into a harmful career path without realizing it, contributing to significant compounding harm over your 80,000 hours of work. It's important to reflect on how you're using this massive resource of time and energy over your life. By doing so, at the very least, you can ensure you are not causing immense harm through your career, and, at best, you could identify ways that would help you to make a significant positive impact. This could be through supporting or working directly for high-impact nonprofits. Other potential high-impact career paths include government policy, research, advocacy careers, or even starting up your own new influential or high-impact organizations.

Each category in the SDAC framework can stack together to have a multiplier effect, compounding the good one can do. Often, progress in one category can help us do better in others. For example, by becoming vegan, you are better suited to be an effective animal welfare advocate. By building skills and finding a beneficial high-paying medical job, you could not only directly work on delivering helpful services but also earn higher wages, thereby enabling you to donate more to high-impact charities. Each category of the SDAC framework reveals that we have the agency to use our unique powers to make a real difference in addressing pressing problems. By carefully reflecting on our privileges and how we can utilize them through these categories, we can put ourselves in a position to be part of the world's solutions rather than part of the world's problems.

7.4 Applying effective altruism concepts to anything

Hopefully after reading this book, you now have a greater understanding of effective altruism as a movement and its underlying concepts. However, you might not identify as an effective altruist or agree with some of the common conclusions the movement has come to, such as the cause areas effective altruists tend to focus on. Effective altruists tend to prioritize areas such as addressing extreme global poverty, improving animal welfare, and mitigating catastrophic risks. Perhaps there are other problem areas you are more concerned about or feel you are better suited to work on. Nonetheless, even if you do not identify as an effective altruist, the tools and frameworks we have explored here can help any individual make the world a better place.

At the end of his book *Doing Good Better*, MacAskill provides five key questions to help explore ways to improve the world for aspiring effective altruists. These questions can help summarize some key effective altruist ideas while also providing important considerations for anybody who wants to do good, whether they identify as an effective altruist or not. The five questions are: (1) How many people benefit and by how much? (2) Is this the most effective thing you can do? (3) Is this area neglected? (4) What would have happened otherwise? (5) What are the chances of success, and how good would success be?[10]

These questions can be seen as an application of the SNS framework (scale, neglectedness, and solvability). The first two help us to gain a sense of the scale and importance of the effects of our actions. Considering how many people can benefit helps us understand the scope of our available actions, especially compared to alternatives. In a world with countless problems, asking whether an option is the most effective thing you can do can help narrow down where to focus your limited time and resources. As explored in Chapter 2, one way to do this when deciding where to donate is to attempt to estimate the cost-effectiveness of your money – what good will result from your donation, and how that compares with donating the same amount elsewhere. This is a useful consideration for any use of your money. What value are you or someone else getting from your purchase compared to what you would spend that money on otherwise?

You can also think of cost-effectiveness not just as being about money but also in terms of the time you invest in an activity. This can apply to all aspects of your life, whether it's volunteering, leisure time, or your career. What do you or others get from the time you devote to a task or activity compared to other uses of that time? We often get stuck in "attention traps" where we may spend an enormous amount of time on an activity or project that gives little to no benefit to anyone in return. Valuing your time and resources is an important concept that can be applied whether or not you consider yourself an effective altruist. By reflecting on how we use our time and what good comes out of our activities compared to available alternatives, we can better allocate our energies to provide a more fulfilling life for ourselves and others.

The next two questions are related: is this area neglected, and what would have happened otherwise? Many of the world's problems have already received enormous attention and funding. Devoting your time and resources to add your support may not make much, or any, difference, given the existing resources already directed at the issue. However, there are problems out there that are not getting the attention and resources they deserve, given their scale and solvability. It's often these neglected areas where your efforts can make a meaningful difference, doing what wouldn't have happened

Making a Difference through Effective Altruism 181

otherwise. This involves "counterfactual thinking" – considering how the world would be different if you took alternative actions. In some cases, the world looks more or less the same regardless of your choice, but in others your actions make a real difference by doing something that otherwise wouldn't have occurred.

While this book has covered many of the global issues that effective altruists view as neglected, this is by no means an exhaustive treatment. Problems can be neglected on many levels, from global to local to individual. In our everyday lives, many problems would be neglected if we didn't address them, like taking care of ourselves, our family, and our friends. If we don't attend to our everyday needs, they may not get met at all. For example, if you don't take yourself to the doctor when sick, no one else will do it for you. This illustrates an important point – while many effective altruist concepts covered in this book apply to large global issues, they can also be helpful in our personal lives. It's important to consider neglectedness and what would happen otherwise, not only for global priorities but also for our everyday lives. Moreover, these spheres can work together – taking good care of yourself and your surroundings can put you in a better position to be more helpful to the broader global community.

The final question relates to solvability – what are the chances of success, and how good would success be? As explored in Chapter 3, we live in an uncertain world and can never be entirely sure of the effects of our actions. However, some tools can help us reduce uncertainty and better understand the landscape of the probabilities we face. As we saw, one such tool is expected value – attempting to assign relative probabilities and value weights to potential outcomes. Addressing uncertainty and acknowledging the world's complexity while directly confronting potential risks and rewards can lead to a more thoughtful and measured approach to improving what's around us.

This careful consideration of probabilities and values of outcomes can help us identify actions that are more likely to do good, while also helping us not dismiss unlikely scenarios with potentially immense impact. Embracing uncertainty thoughtfully, rather than ignoring it, can help us avoid dismissing low-probability events when high stakes are involved. Some activities may not be likely to make a difference, but they are still important to consider, because their impact would be so immense if they did occur. As explored with moral caution in Chapter 3, this can mean giving more consideration to potential moral risks and taking uncertainty into account when making significant decisions.

Acknowledging the uncertainty and complexity of our world can be a helpful approach in our everyday lives. Very often, we tend toward overconfidence and oversimplification. Taking uncertainty into account in our daily actions, especially our most significant choices, can encourage thoughtful reflection on the impacts of our decisions and better represent the complexity of the world around us. It can also help us to have more fruitful discussions with those that we disagree with.

This leads to an important consideration for the various frameworks and arguments explored in this book. Rather than seeing them as hard and fast rules that must be followed, it is better to view them as helpful tools that can improve our thinking and decision-making. Instead of strict edicts, things like MacAskill's list of questions or the SNS framework can serve as ways to think about the world that can improve our judgment and hopefully help us make a greater positive difference.

Even if you don't identify as an effective altruist after reading this book, hopefully you found some of the ideas and arguments helpful for improving your path to making the world a better place. Even if you aren't working on what effective altruists would consider the most high-impact cause areas, you can still look for ways to have an outsized positive change. It's better to view the impact as a spectrum rather than simply as being high or low. There is a wide variety of ways we can do good in the world. Even for small-scale causes, individuals can still focus on the biggest ways they personally can do to make a positive difference within those domains. As such, studying effective altruist concepts can help anyone looking to increase their positive impact. In other words, the basic methods explored in this book could be helpful for anyone seeking to do good better, regardless of whether they identify specifically as an effective altruist.

For those that do resonate with effective altruism, the next section provides some recommendations on what you can do next.

7.5 Taking the next steps: Becoming more effective altruists

For those inspired by the effective altruism movement, here are four recommended steps to further your journey to becoming a more effective altruist: (1) Join a community; (2) learn more; (3) talk to others; and (4) put theory into action.

The first recommendation is to join an effective altruist community. Although effective altruism is still a young movement, there are many communities within it to pick from. Getting involved in a group can help you gain connections, learn about the latest developments on current issues, and find like-minded friends. Joining a community can also open up opportunities and career pathways to do even more good with your time. As we have seen, groups can also help coordinate collective action to achieve more than individuals can alone.

You might have a local effective altruism group nearby. You can search a list of local groups online at the Effective Altruism Forum (https://forum.effectivealtruism.org/groups). If there are no groups near you, you can find other resources to start your own local community and begin building a network of effective altruists near you (https://eagroups.org/). There are dozens of online effective altruism groups, including reading groups, groups centered on effective giving, religion-based groups such as Effective Altruism for Christians, and groups focused on specific cause areas like AI safety, biosecurity, animal advocacy, and environmentalism.

The Effective Altruism Forum also hosts an active online community of individuals sharing thoughts and research on topics of common interest. Another way to engage with the effective altruism community is to apply to attend one of the numerous "Effective Altruism Global" conferences that take place across the world and online each year.[11] Finding the right community can help you gain like-minded friends who care about making a difference and can boost your learning about the latest developments on how to best help address pressing problems.

This leads us to the next recommendation: learning more about effective altruism concepts and high-impact ways to address the world's most pressing problems. This book is only an introduction. There is a wealth of information available on each topic covered here, with new research and organizations emerging each year. Keeping up with current developments is important to know where your efforts can be best applied. At the end of this chapter is an annotated list of helpful resources for those who want to dive deeper.

The next recommendation is to talk to others about effective altruism. Although joining groups and communities helps facilitate this, it's also valuable to share the ideas you have found compelling in this book with people in your life outside the effective altruism community. It's good to share your insights with others, as well as spread potentially useful ideas. It's also valuable to discuss these concepts with non-effective altruists to get outside input and feedback to refine your own views.

Conversations help clarify your own thinking and encourage you to better articulate your beliefs on important issues. Constructive discussion with others enables you to improve ideas where needed and reject those that do not hold up to scrutiny. By openly communicating with others, you can continually refine your thinking and avoid potential pitfalls, putting yourself in a better position to use your time, energy, and resources to more effectively improve the world. Conversations may also open up new opportunities for you and others to have a greater positive impact.

The final and potentially most important recommendation is putting theory into action. Of course, it's important to learn and continually improve your beliefs on how to have an impact. But these beliefs only matter if acted upon. The only way to make a difference is to take concrete steps. This means periodically setting time aside to reflect on how you can make a difference and make commitments on how to implement those ideas. For example, this could involve setting up a monthly donation to effective charities. Giving What We Can provides resources to help research and assess what you believe are the highest-impact charities, set up recurring donations, and make it easy to update your giving.

Another option relating to high-impact charity is to sign one of the public giving pledge commitments. Many effective altruists take the Giving What We Can pledge to give 10 percent of their income to top charities. They also have other pledges, including a trial pledge of any percentage of 1 percent or above, if you want to try it out before making a larger commitment. The Life You Can Save also has a giving pledge, starting at 1 percent for lower incomes, and increasing with higher earnings.

If you're interested in high-impact career paths, both 80,000 Hours and Probably Good offer many resources to help individuals direct their professional lives toward making a positive difference in the world. You could start by setting aside time each week to read and reflect on portions of their career guides. When you're ready, you could apply for additional one-on-one career advice.

The key is to start somewhere and then build commitment over time. Take the ideas that resonate with you and put them into meaningful action, in whatever domain you feel compelled to contribute to. Hopefully, this book has provided many options to consider in how you can help make the world a better place. By studying effective altruism, you have gained a greater understanding of this movement's core ideas and insights into how you can have an impact. At a certain point, we must move beyond just thinking about improving the world to actually putting ideas into action and learning from the results.

This book covered a variety of concepts, frameworks, and examples for being more helpful to others. There are always more ways we can learn about the world's problems and solutions. As we learn more, it's important that we also find opportunities to apply that knowledge to make a positive change. Although no one person can solve all the immense global issues we face, each of us has the power to be part of real solutions to some of them. Hopefully, this book has helped you recognize the "superpowers" you have and how you can harness them responsibly to help others.

This book is meant only as an introduction to effective altruism; it marks just the beginning of a fruitful investigation into how each of us can become more effective with our altruism. The challenge now is to take what you've absorbed, reflect carefully on your unique talents and situation, and then take concrete steps to create a better world. What resonated with you from the ideas and examples we explored? How might you translate that inspiration into practical action? There's no one right way to do this. Try to discover what genuine contributions you are uniquely suited in this world to make. With careful reasoning, assessment of evidence, openness, and creativity, we all have the power to make a difference. Let's use that power wisely.

Questions for reflection

1. What do you think of effective altruism? What are some of the strengths and weaknesses of the movement, based on what you have learned from this book? What concepts would you like to learn more about?

2. What are some of the altruistic superpowers that you currently have? Which ones are you likely to develop in the future? How can you use those powers to benefit the world?
3. What aspects of the SDAC framework seem most promising for you to pursue right now? What are some that you can work on pursuing in the future? What are some of the biggest ways that you personally can improve the world over the course of your life?
4. What effective altruist concepts do you think are useful in everyday life? Explain, using examples.

Classroom exercise

Write down a few key takeaways from this book that you think will be most useful in improving your own life and the lives of others. Develop a plan on how you can implement some of these ideas. List specific, achievable action items for yourself over varying timeframes – today, this week, next year, next five years, a lifetime. Discuss your plan with others and get feedback.

Helpful resources

Podcasts

- *80,000 Hours*. This podcast features in-depth conversations about the world's most pressing problems and possible solutions. For those new to effective altruism, this podcast offers a compilation of its top ten episodes, titled "Effective Altruism: An Introduction. A Compilation from 80,000 Hours."
- *Clearer Thinking with Spencer Greenberg*. This podcast explores a wide range of topics, including psychology,

philosophy, science, mathematics, and AI, offering insights relevant to effective altruism.
- *Hear This Idea.* Hosted by Finn Morehouse and Luca Righetti, this podcast explores topics related to effective altruism, philosophy, and the social sciences.
- *Cold Takes.* Holden Karnofsky, mentioned in this book, hosts this insightful podcast on topics ranging from global poverty to existential risks from AI.
- *The Future of Life Institute Podcast.* This podcast presents discussions with experts on mitigating global catastrophic risks.

Online courses

- *Introduction to Effective Altruism by Peter Singer on Coursera.* This free course includes more than forty short videos, providing an accessible entry point into the principles of effective altruism, especially as related to global poverty. https://www.coursera.org/learn/altruism.
- *Introductory EA Program.* This eight-week course runs several times a year and allows you to learn more about the key ideas of effective altruism in a virtual small-group setting. After completing this course, there is an additional "In-Depth EA Program" eight-week course available. https://www.effectivealtruism.org/virtual-programs.

Books

Doing Good Better, by William MacAskill, and *The Most Good You Can Do*, by Peter Singer. Both published in 2015, these early works on effective altruism focus on high-impact giving.

80,000 Hours: Find a Fulfilling Career That Does Good by Benjamin Todd (2023). This career guide to high-impact careers is available in paper form and also online on the 80,000 Hours webpage.

The Precipice, by Toby Ord (2020) and *What We Owe the Future*, by William MacAskill (2022). These books explore existential risks and longtermism.

The Life You Can Save, by Peter Singer (2019). This book emphasizes doing what we can to help those living in extreme poverty through high-impact giving.

Videos

- Centre for Effective Altruism YouTube Channel. This houses hundreds of talks from Effective Altruism Global conferences, including the most recent ones and those dating back to 2016. These videos provide an excellent way to stay up to date with current developments in effective altruism and related research areas. https://www.youtube.com/c/EffectiveAltruismVideos.
- TED Talks: There are numerous TED videos on effective altruism and related topics. Notable videos include:
  - "The why and how of effective altruism," by Peter Singer (2013). https://www.ted.com/speakers/peter_singer.
  - "What are the most important moral problems of our time?," by William MacAskill (2018). https://www.ted.com/speakers/will_macaskill.
  - "How to save hundreds of lives," by Toby Ord (2014). https://www.youtube.com/watch?v=ZGAkrpwyu1k.
  - "To find work you love, don't follow your passion," by Benjamin Todd (2015). https://www.youtube.com/watch?v=MKlx1DLa9EA.
  - "The 4 greatest threats to the survival of humanity," by TED-Ed (2022). https://www.ted.com/talks/ted_ed_the_4_greatest_threats_to_the_survival_of_humanity.
  - "What if you experienced every human life in history?," by TED-Ed (2023). https://www.ted.com/talks/ted_ed_what_if_you_experienced_every_human_life_in_history.

Additional resources

- "Take Action," *Effective Altruism*. A detailed list of dozens of ways to have an impact and become more involved in the effective altruism community. https://www.effectivealtruism.org/get-involved.
- Effective Altruism resource page, https://www.effectivealtruism.org/resources/videos; 80,000 Hours further resources page, https://80000hours.org/articles/further-reading/. These offer dozens more resources on effective altruism, including introductory materials, in-depth discussions, and the latest developments in the field.

Notes

Introduction: What is Effective Altruism?
1. For a very brief introduction to effective altruism, see Jacob Bauer, "What's Effective Altruism? A Philosopher Explains," *The Conversation*, January 26, 2023, http://theconversation.com/whats-effective-altruism-a-philosopher-explains-197856.
2. William MacAskill, "The Definition of Effective Altruism," in Hilary Greaves and Theron Pummer, eds., *Effective Altruism: Philosophical Issues* (Oxford: Oxford University Press, 2019), 12. William MacAskill, "The History of the Term 'Effective Altruism,'" EA Forum, March 11, 2014, https://forum.effectivealtruism.org/posts/9a7xMXoSiQs3EYPA2/the-history-of-the-term-effective-altruism.
3. See Centre for Effective Altruism, "History": https://www.centreforeffectivealtruism.org/history. These nonprofits include Giving What We Can in 2009, followed by 80,000 Hours, and an umbrella organization, The Centre for Effective Altruism, in 2011.
4. Michel Justen, "A Database of EA Organizations & Initiatives," EA Forum, July 22, 2022, https://forum.effectivealtruism.org/posts/wLZExunpNhAnafJbg/a-database-of-ea-organizations-and-initiatives. "EA&EA: Adjacent Organizations," EA Opportunities, n.d., https://ea-internships.pory.app/orgs. Benjamin Todd, "How Are Resources in Effective Altruism Allocated across Issues?" 80,000 Hours, August 9, 2021, https://80000hours.org/2021/08/effective-altruism-allocation-resources-cause-areas/.

Chapter 1: The Urgency of Effective Altruism: Pandemics and Prioritization

1. Benedetta Armocida et al., "The Italian Health System and the COVID-19 Challenge," *The Lancet Public Health* 5, no. 5 (May 1, 2020), e253, https://doi.org/10.1016/S2468-2667(20)30074-8. Advisory Board, "How Coronavirus Overwhelmed One of Italy's Premier Hospitals," March 20, 2023, https://www.advisory.com/daily-briefing/2020/03/19/italian-hospitals. Guglielmo Gianotti, "I'm a Doctor at Italy's Hardest-Hit Hospital. I Had to Decide Who Got a Ventilator and Who Didn't," *ABC News*, March 26, 2020, https://www.abc.net.au/news/2020-03-27/coronavirus-doctor-cremona-hospital-decide-who-lives-and-dies/12090912.
2. Harrison Jones, "Italian Doctor's Stark Coronavirus Warning as He's Forced to Choose Who Lives," *Metro*, March 24, 2020, sec. News, https://metro.co.uk/2020/03/24/italian-doctors-stark-coronavirus-warning-forced-choose-lives-12449509/.
3. Yascha Mounk, "The Extraordinary Decisions Facing Italian Doctors," *The Atlantic*, March 11, 2020, sec. Ideas, https://www.theatlantic.com/ideas/archive/2020/03/who-gets-hospital-bed/607807/.
4. Charles C. Yancey and Maria C. O'Rourke, "Emergency Department Triage," in *StatPearls* (Treasure Island, FL: StatPearls Publishing, 2023), http://www.ncbi.nlm.nih.gov/books/NBK557583/.
5. Importance/Tractability/Crowdedness (ITC) in 2013 by Holden Karnofsky (GiveWell Labs/Open Philanthropy), Scale/Neglectedness/Tractability (SNT) in 2014 by Owen Cotton-Barratt (Future of Humanity Institute), Importance/Tractability/Neglectedness (ITN) in 2015 by Holden Karnofsky (Open Philanthropy), Scale/Neglectedness/Solvability (SNS) in 2016 by Robert Wiblin and Benjamin Todd (80,000 Hours). William MacAskill used SNT in *Doing Good Better: How Effective Altruism Can Help You Make a Difference* (New York: Gotham Books, 2015) and ITN in *What We Owe The Future* (New York: Basic Books, 2022). Given the accessibility of the terms, SNS is used in this chapter; however, ITN is becoming more popular in effective altruist literature. For more on the history of the framework, see EA Forum, "ITN Framework," n.d., https://forum.effectivealtruism.org/topics

/itn-framework; Luke Muehlhauser, "Holden Karnofsky on Transparent Research Analyses," Machine Intelligence Research Institute, August 25, 2013, https://intelligence.org/2013/08/25/holden-karnofsky-interview/; Holden Karnofsky, "Narrowing down U.S. Policy Areas," *Open Philanthropy* (blog), May 22, 2014, https://www.openphilanthropy.org/research/narrowing-down-u-s-policy-areas/; Owen Cotton-Barratt, "Estimating Cost-Effectiveness for Problems of Unknown Difficulty," Future of Humanity Institute, December 4, 2014, https://www.fhi.ox.ac.uk/estimating-cost-effectiveness/; Robert Wiblin, "A Framework for Comparing Global Problems in Terms of Expected Impact," 80,000 Hours, 2016, https://80000hours.org/articles/problem-framework/; Benjamin Todd, *80,000 Hours: Find a Fulfilling Career That Does Good*, First printing (Oxford: Centre for Effective Altruism, 2016), 50–6; Probably Good, "Analyzing Cause Areas," n.d., https://probablygood.org/career-guide/analyzing-cause-areas/; Open Philanthropy, "Focus Areas," June 30, 2021, https://www.openphilanthropy.org/focus/; MacAskill, *Doing Good Better*, 181; MacAskill, *What We Owe the Future*, 256.

6 Developed in part by the organization 80,000 Hours. See Todd, *80,000 Hours*, 50–6.

7 These questions are based on similar ones from Benjamin Todd, "Want to Do Good? Here's How to Choose an Area to Focus on," 80,000 Hours, https://80000hours.org/career-guide/most-pressing-problems/. The terms are inspired by Jeremy Bentham's felicific calculus; see James E. Crimmins, "Jeremy Bentham," in Edward N. Zalta and Uri Nodelman, eds., *The Stanford Encyclopedia of Philosophy*, Fall 2023 (Metaphysics Research Lab, Stanford University, 2023), https://plato.stanford.edu/archives/fall2023/entries/bentham/.

8 START (National Consortium for the Study of Terrorism and Responses to Terrorism), "Global Terrorism Database 1970–2020 [Data File]," 2022, https://www.start.umd.edu/gtd. The number of people killed from terrorism between 1970 and 2020 was approximately 479,000.

9 As of June 25, 2023, *The Economist* central excess death estimate from COVID-19 was 23.8 million, with lower bound of 17 million and upper bound of 30.8 million. A conservative estimate of 20 million was given based on this data. *The*

Economist, "The Pandemic's True Death Toll," June 26, 2023, https://www.economist.com/graphic-detail/coronavirus-excess-deaths-estimates. This comparison is inspired by Centre for Effective Altruism, "What Is Effective Altruism?," n.d., https://www.effectivealtruism.org/articles/introduction-to-effective-altruism#preventing-the-next-pandemic.

10 These estimates are from Centre for Effective Altruism, "What Is Effective Altruism?" See note 3 from that article for how the annual estimates were derived using data from C. Watson et al., "Federal Funding for Health Security in FY2019," *Health Security* 16 (October 17, 2018), 281–303; Neta C. Crawford, "The U.S. Budgetary Costs of the Post-9/11 Wars through FY2022," https://watson.brown.edu/costsofwar/figures/2021/BudgetaryCosts.

11 This set of questions is adapted from section 2 of Todd, "Want to Do Good?"

12 Brendon Sen-Crowe, Mark McKenney, and Adel Elkbuli, "Public Health Prevention and Emergency Preparedness Funding in the United States: Are We Ready for the Next Pandemic?," *Annals of Medicine and Surgery* 59 (October 10, 2020), 242–4, https://doi.org/10.1016/j.amsu.2020.10.007.

13 Donald G. McNeil Jr, "Scientists Were Hunting for the Next Ebola. Now the U.S. Has Cut Off Their Funding," *New York Times*, October 25, 2019, sec. Health, https://www.nytimes.com/2019/10/25/health/predict-usaid-viruses.html.

14 Kayla Epstein, "The Trump Administration Stopped Funding a Pandemic Warning Program Just a Few Months before the Novel Coronavirus Outbreak," *Business Insider*, April 3, 2020, https://www.businessinsider.com/us-cut-pandemic-warning-project-before-coronavirus-outbreak-2020-4.

15 This set of questions is adapted from section 3 of Todd, "Want to Do Good?"

16 See World Health Organization, *World Report on Vision* (Geneva: World Health Organization, 2019), https://apps.who.int/iris/handle/10665/328717; The Life You Can Save, "Seva Foundation," n.d., https://www.thelifeyoucansave.org/best-charities/seva/.

17 See MacAskill, *Doing Good Better*, Ch. 10; Todd, *80,000 Hours*, Ch. 3; and Wiblin, "A Framework for Comparing Global Problems," sec. 9.

18 For more on problem areas effective altruists work on,

see 80,000 Hours, "What Are the Most Pressing World Problems?," May 24, 2023, https://80000hours.org/problem-profiles/; Open Philanthropy, "Focus Areas"; and Probably Good, "Important Cause Areas," n.d., https://probablygood.org/career-guide/important-cause-areas/. For an estimation on the allocation of effective altruist funding toward each problem in 2019, see Todd, "How Are Resources in Effective Altruism Allocated across Issues?"

19 Emma Marris, "The Trouble with Algorithmic Ethics," *Sierra Magazine*, Summer 2023.
20 William MacAskill, "Moral Progress and Cause X," October 7, 2016, https://www.effectivealtruism.org/articles/moral-progress-and-cause-x; EA Forum, "Cause X," n.d., https://forum.effectivealtruism.org/topics/cause-x.
21 See Roman Duda, "Global Priorities Research," 80,000 Hours, June 21, 2023, https://80000hours.org/problem-profiles/global-priorities-research/.
22 World Health Organization, "The True Death Toll of COVID-19: Estimating Global Excess Mortality," n.d., https://www.who.int/data/stories/the-true-death-toll-of-covid-19-estimating-global-excess-mortality; Edouard Mathieu et al., "Excess Mortality during the Coronavirus Pandemic (COVID-19)," *Our World in Data*, March 5, 2020, https://ourworldindata.org/excess-mortality-covid; Megan Crigger and Laura Santhanam, "How Many Americans Have Died in U.S. Wars?," *PBS NewsHour*, May 24, 2015, https://www.pbs.org/newshour/nation/many-americans-died-u-s-wars; Statista, "United States: War Fatalities 1775–2023," n.d., https://www.statista.com/statistics/1009819/total-us-military-fatalities-in-american-wars-1775-present/.
23 Rachel E. Baker et al., "Infectious Disease in an Era of Global Change," *Nature Reviews Microbiology* 20, no. 4 (April 2022), 193–205, https://doi.org/10.1038/s41579-021-00639-z.
24 Romain Espinosa, Damian Tago, and Nicolas Treich, "Infectious Diseases and Meat Production," *Environmental and Resource Economics* 76, no. 4 (August 2020), 1019–44, https://doi.org/10.1007/s10640-020-00484-3.
25 Amber Dance, "The Shifting Sands of 'Gain-of-Function' Research," *Nature* 598, no. 7882 (October 27, 2021), 554–7, https://doi.org/10.1038/d41586-021-02903-x.

26 Michael J. Selgelid, "Gain-of-Function Research: Ethical Analysis," *Science and Engineering Ethics* 22, no. 4 (August 2016), 923–64, https://doi.org/10.1007/s11948-016-9810-1. For a list of notable lab escapes of pathogens, see Toby Ord, *The Precipice: Existential Risk and the Future of Humanity* (New York: Hachette Books, 2020), 131.

27 For more recommendations, see Arden Koehler and Benjamin Hilton, "Preventing Catastrophic Pandemics," 80,000 Hours, December 2023, https://80000hours.org/problem-profiles/preventing-catastrophic-pandemics/; Giving What We Can, "Improving Biosecurity and Pandemic Preparedness," n.d., https://www.givingwhatwecan.org/cause-areas/long-term-future/biosecurity.

Chapter 2: Global Poverty: You CAN Make a Difference

1 Max Roser, "The World Is Awful. The World Is Much Better. The World Can Be Much Better," Our World in Data, February 2024, https://ourworldindata.org/much-better-awful-can-be-better.

2 The estimated global number of annual child deaths is 5.86 million. The global average child mortality rate in low-income countries is 4.4%, more than seven times higher than that of high-income countries (0.6%). Only 0.8 million would die if the average global mortality rate was 0.6% instead of 4.4% (5.86 million / (4.4 / 0.6) ≈ 0.8 million). This is 5.06 million fewer children each year, 13,860 per day. This is inspired by a similar calculation found in Roser, "The World Is Awful." If the global mortality rate was the same as in low-income countries, 8.1%, almost 11 million children would die each year, 5 million more than today (5.86 million / (4.4 / 8.1)). Based on the most recent youth mortality rates available at the time of writing, 2021; see Our World in Data, "Youth Mortality Rate," August 16, 2023, https://ourworldindata.org/grapher/youth-mortality-rate.

3 The worst jumbo jet accident so far this century killed 298 people, in 2014. Aviation Safety Network, "100 Worst Aviation Accidents," n.d., https://aviation-safety.net/statistics/worst/worst.php?list=worstcoll.

4 Max Roser, "Extreme Poverty: How Far Have We Come, How Far Do We Still Have to Go?," *Our World in Data*, August 27, 2023, https://ourworldindata.org/extreme-poverty-in-brief.

5 Ruth Hill, Christoph Lakner, et al., "Poverty, Median Incomes, and Inequality in 2021: A Diverging Recovery," Washington, DC: World Bank Group, 2021, http://documents.worldbank.org/curated/en/936001635880885713/Poverty-Median-Incomes-and-Inequality-in-2021-A-Diverging-Recovery.

6 Joe Hasell et al., "Explore Data on Poverty," *Our World in Data*, July 18, 2023, https://ourworldindata.org/poverty#explore-data-on-poverty.

7 U.S. Bureau of Labor Statistics, "Education Pays," n.d., https://www.bls.gov/emp/chart-unemployment-earnings-education.htm.

8 GiveWell, "Our Story," n.d., https://www.givewell.org/about/story.

9 Giving What We Can, "Our History," n.d., https://www.givingwhatwecan.org/about-us/history.

10 These numbers are from "Calculate the Impact You Can Have," The Life You Can Save, n.d., https://www.thelifeyoucansave.org/impact-calculator/.

11 GiveWell, "GiveDirectly – November 2020 Version," November 2020, https://www.givewell.org/charities/give-directly/November-2020-version; Giving What We Can, "GiveDirectly," n.d., https://www.givingwhatwecan.org/charities/givedirectly.

12 Elie Hassenfeld, "Changes to Our Top Charity Criteria, and a New Giving Option," *GiveWell* (blog), August 17, 2022, https://blog.givewell.org/2022/08/17/changes-to-top-charity-criteria/.

13 These lists are regularly updated. In addition to these four, at the time of writing, Giving What We Can also recommends the following as top-rated charities: Iodine Global Network, Lead Exposure Elimination Project, StrongMinds, Suvita, and Teaching at the Right Level Africa. For their current top recommendations, see GiveWell, "Our Top Charities," n.d., https://www.givewell.org/charities/top-charities; Giving What We Can, "High-Impact Charities and Nonprofits," n.d., https://www.givingwhatwecan.org/donate/organizations.

14 For more on this style of objection, see Travis Timmerman, "Sometimes There Is Nothing Wrong with Letting a Child Drown," *Analysis* 75, no. 2 (2015), 204–12.

15 Bureau of Labor Statistics, "May 2022 National Occupational

Employment and Wage Estimates," April 25, 2023, https://www.bls.gov/oes/current/oes_nat.htm.

16 William MacAskill, "To Save the World, Don't Get a Job at a Charity; Go Work on Wall Street," *Quartz*, February 27, 2013, https://qz.com/57254/to-save-the-world-dont-get-a-job-at-a-charity-go-work-on-wall-street.

17 This isn't a universal rule, as some charities may be in greater need of workers than of funding and you might be particularly well suited to make a larger impact in one of those roles. See Chapter 5 for more on high-impact careers.

18 Jonathan Meer and Benjamin Priday, "Generosity Across the Income and Wealth Distributions" (Cambridge, MA: National Bureau of Economic Research, May 2020), 29, https://doi.org/10.3386/w27076.

19 "Sam Bankman-Fried," Forbes, n.d., https://www.forbes.com/profile/sam-bankman-fried/.

20 Benjamin Todd and William MacAskill, "Why You Should Avoid Harmful Jobs, Even If You'll Do More Good," 80,000 Hours, June 2017, https://80000hours.org/articles/harmful-career/.

21 MacAskill, *Doing Good Better*, 3–5.

22 For a more detailed account of this objection and many others, see Larry S. Temkin, *Being Good in a World of Need* (New York: Oxford University Press, 2022).

23 For an example of this, see Holden Karnofsky, "Evidence of Impact for Long-Term Benefits," GiveWell (blog), July 25, 2016, https://blog.givewell.org/2012/12/14/evidence-of-impact-for-long-term-benefits/.

24 Peter Singer, "The Singer Solution To World Poverty," *New York Times*, September 5, 1999, sec. Magazine, https://www.nytimes.com/1999/09/05/magazine/the-singer-solution-to-world-poverty.html.

25 "Our Giving Funds," GiveWell, n.d., https://www.givewell.org/our-giving-funds; "Expert Managed Charitable Funds," Giving What We Can, n.d., https://www.givingwhatwecan.org/donate/organizations.

26 In 2022, William MacAskill's reported giving level is everything over £26,000 post-tax. In 2023, Toby Ord, in correspondence with the author, reported living on £27,025 for himself (not including spending on dependents), and donating the rest to

poverty-related charities. Based on currency conversion rates at the time of writing, this is around US$33,000–35,000. For publications that discuss their giving, see Naina Bajekal, "Inside the Growing Movement to Do the Most Good Possible," *Time*, August 10, 2022, https://time.com/6204627/effective-altruism-longtermism-william-macaskill-interview/; Dylan Matthews, "This Man Has Donated at Least 10% of His Salary to Charity for 11 Years Running," *Vox*, November 30, 2020, https://www.vox.com/future-perfect/21728925/charity-10-percent-tithe-giving-what-we-can-toby-ord.

27 Giving What We Can, "Our Pledge," n.d., https://www.givingwhatwecan.org/pledge.

28 Freeman outlines numerous other possible giving standards as well as some giving recommendations; see his "How Much Money Should We Donate to Charity?," May 27, 2021, https://www.givingwhatwecan.org/blog/how-much-money-should-we-donate-to-charity.

29 Freeman, "How Much Money Should We Donate to Charity?"

30 Max Roser, "Mortality in the Past: Every Second Child Died," Our World in Data, April 11, 2023, https://ourworldindata.org/child-mortality-in-the-past.

31 Roser, "Extreme Poverty."

32 Benjamin Todd, "Why and How to Earn to Give," 80,000 Hours, March 2023, https://80000hours.org/articles/earning-to-give/.

Chapter 3: Weighing Uncertainties: Should You Be Vegan?

1 According to a 2019 survey of the effective altruism community, more than 46% identified as a vegetarian or vegan. In comparison, only 2–6% of Americans identify as vegetarian. Neil Dullaghan, "EA Survey 2019: Community Demographics & Characteristics," Rethink Priorities, December 5, 2019, https://rethinkpriorities.org/publications/eas2019-community-demographics-characteristics; Saulius Šimčikas, "Is the Percentage of Vegetarians and Vegans in the U.S. Increasing?," *Animal Charity Evaluators* (blog), August 16, 2018, https://animalcharityevaluators.org/blog/is-the-percentage-of-vegetarians-and-vegans-in-the-u-s-increasing/.

2 Section 3.1, including arguments regarding moral catastrophes, inductive worry, disjunctive worry, and claims of complicity,

draws upon ideas and analysis from Evan G. Williams, "The Possibility of an Ongoing Moral Catastrophe," *Ethical Theory and Moral Practice* 18, no. 5 (November 1, 2015), 971–82. For an excellent outline summary of the paper, see Linchuan Zhang, "The Possibility of an Ongoing Moral Catastrophe (Summary)," August 2, 2019, https://forum.effectivealtruism.org/posts/Dtr8aHqCQSDhyueFZ/the-possibility-of-an-ongoing-moral-catastrophe-summary.

3 "Two thousand years ago, the Romans – the *imperialistic, crucifying, slave-owning* Romans – were congratulating themselves on being 'civilized,' because unlike the 'barbarians' they had abolished human sacrifice": Williams, "The Possibility of an Ongoing Moral Catastrophe," p. 974.

4 Sentience Institute, "99% of US Farmed Animals Live on Factory Farms, Study Shows," Sentience Institute, April 11, 2019, http://www.sentienceinstitute.org/press/us-farmed-animals-live-on-factory-farms.

5 Hannah Ritchie, Pablo Rosado, and Max Roser, "Meat and Dairy Production," *Our World in Data*, December 2023, https://ourworldindata.org/meat-production.

6 Ritchie et al., "Meat and Dairy Production."

7 Other alternatives to anthropocentrism include biocentrism, ecocentrism, and value pluralism; however, these are more relevant to broader discussions within environmental ethics. See Marion Hourdequin, *Environmental Ethics: From Theory to Practice* (London: Bloomsbury Academic, 2015), Ch. 3.

8 For more on the principle of equality and speciesism, see Peter Singer, *Animal Liberation Now* (New York: Harper Perennial, 2023), Ch. 1.

9 See Singer, *Animal Liberation Now*, Ch. 1.

10 For a brief overview of Regan's animal rights view, see Tom Regan, "The Case for Animal Rights," in Michael W. Fox and Linda D. Mickley, eds., *Advances in Animal Welfare Science 1986/87* (Dordrecht: Springer Netherlands, 1987), 179–89, https://doi.org/10.1007/978-94-009-3331-6_15. For a more comprehensive treatment, see Tom Regan, *The Case for Animal Rights*, 2nd ed. (Berkeley: University of California Press, 2004).

11 William MacAskill, Krister Bykvist, and Toby Ord, *Moral Uncertainty* (New York: Oxford University Press, 2020), 11–14.

12. Pauline Austin Adams and Joe K. Adams, "Confidence in the Recognition and Reproduction of Words Difficult to Spell," *The American Journal of Psychology* 73, no. 4 (December 1960), 544.
13. Other approaches to moral uncertainty include the parliamentary model and normative externalism. For a brief overview, see EA Forum, "Moral Uncertainty," n.d., https://forum.effectivealtruism.org/topics/moral-uncertainty.
14. For a brief introduction to moral uncertainty and moral caution, see Benjamin Todd, "Moral Uncertainty: How to Act When You're Uncertain about What's Good," 80,000 Hours, September 2021, https://80000hours.org/articles/moral-uncertainty/.
15. For a more detailed account, see William MacAskill, "Practical Ethics Given Moral Uncertainty," *Utilitas* 31, no. 3 (September 2019), 231–45.
16. Hossein Pishro-Nik, *Introduction to Probability, Statistics, and Random Processes* (Blue Bell, PA: Kappa Research, LLC, 2014), 377.
17. The typical expected value of a bet at a casino ranges from $-0.01 to -0.10 per dollar wagered. This expected loss is generally called house edge, expressed as a percentage (e.g. 1%–10%). Expected loss can be reduced or increased for some games based on betting strategies. For an interactive tool to explore these concepts, see Michael Bluejay, "Gambling Concepts: Expected Loss," Easy Vegas, January 2022, https://easy.vegas/gambling/average-loss.
18. James P. Whelan, "Millions of Americans Are Problem Gamblers: So Why Do So Few People Ever Seek Treatment?," *The Conversation*, February 8, 2023, http://theconversation.com/millions-of-americans-are-problem-gamblers-so-why-do-so-few-people-ever-seek-treatment-197861.
19. F. Bailey Norwood and Jayson Lusk, *Compassion, by the Pound: The Economics of Farm Animal Welfare* (New York: Oxford University Press, 2011), 222–4, 251–7.
20. Norwood and Lusk, *Compassion, by the Pound*, 230.
21. Using 2020 numbers, according to Our World in Data, "Meat Supply per Person," n.d., https://ourworldindata.org/grapher/meat-supply-per-person.
22. Based on one chicken producing around 5 pounds of meat and

one cow producing around 560 pounds of meat. University of Minnesota Extension, "Buying Animals for Meat Processing," 2020, https://extension.umn.edu/save-money-food/buying-animals-meat-processing.
23 Norwood and Lusk, *Compassion, by the Pound*, 228–9.
24 Ali Ladak, Clara Sanchez Garcia, and Jo Anderson, "The Impact of Replacing Animal Products," Faunalytics, September 16, 2020, https://faunalytics.org/animal-product-impact-scales/.
25 Ladak et al., "The Impact of Replacing Animal Products."
26 Including vegans, vegetarians, pescatarians, and those who identified as trying to reduce the amount of meat they eat, this comes to over 82% of the effective altruist community surveyed in 2019; see Dullaghan, "EA Survey 2019."
27 This leads to a number of more advanced theoretical problems for expected value theory, such as Pascal's Mugging, the St. Petersburg Paradox, and the Gambler's Ruin. While these complex issues are beyond the scope of this introductory text, they are great starting points for those interested in exploring the complexities and limitations of expected value theory further.
28 Holden Karnofsky, "Hits-Based Giving," *Open Philanthropy* (blog), April 4, 2016, https://www.openphilanthropy.org/research/hits-based-giving/.
29 For a discussion of hits-based vs data-driven approaches, see Benjamin Todd, "The Best Solutions Are Far More Effective than Others," 80,000 Hours, September 2021, https://80000hours.org/articles/solutions/.
30 For examples, see Benjamin Todd, "Expected Value: How Can We Make a Difference When We're Uncertain What's True?," 80,000 Hours, April 2023, https://80000hours.org/articles/expected-value/; Centre for Effective Altruism, "Core EA Principles," n.d., https://www.centreforeffectivealtruism.org/core-principles.
31 Roman Duda, "Factory Farming: Why Helping to End Factory Farming Could Be the Most Important Thing You Could Do," 80,000 Hours, February 2022, https://80000hours.org/problem-profiles/factory-farming/; Probably Good, "Animal Welfare," n.d., https://probablygood.org/cause-areas/animal-welfare/.

Chapter 4: Systemic Change and Moral Pitfalls: Combating Climate Change

1. 80,000 Hours, "What Are the Most Pressing World Problems?" May 2023, https://80000hours.org/problem-profiles/.
2. Hannah Ritchie, Pablo Rosado, and Max Roser, "Greenhouse Gas Emissions," *Our World in Data*, January 2024, https://ourworldindata.org/greenhouse-gas-emissions.
3. Rounded up from 17.6 tons in 2021; see Ritchie et al., "Greenhouse Gas Emissions."
4. Nina Lakhani, "Revealed: Top Carbon Offset Projects May Not Cut Planet-Heating Emissions," *Guardian*, September 19, 2023, sec. Environment, https://www.theguardian.com/environment/2023/sep/19/do-carbon-credit-reduce-emissions-greenhouse-gases.
5. Patrick Greenfield, "Revealed: More than 90% of Rainforest Carbon Offsets by Biggest Certifier Are Worthless, Analysis Shows," *Guardian*, January 18, 2023, sec. Environment, https://www.theguardian.com/environment/2023/jan/18/revealed-forest-carbon-offsets-biggest-provider-worthless-verra-aoe.
6. Barbara K. Haya et al., "Comprehensive Review of Carbon Quantification by Improved Forest Management Offset Protocols," *Frontiers in Forests and Global Change* 6 (2023), https://www.frontiersin.org/articles/10.3389/ffgc.2023.958879; "Bogus Carbon Credits a 'Pervasive' Problem, Scientists Warn," *Time*, March 21, 2023, https://time.com/6264772/study-most-carbon-credits-are-bogus/.
7. "About Giving Green," Giving Green, n.d., https://www.givinggreen.earth/about-us.
8. Christian Turney, Lennart Bach, and Philip Boyd, "Carbon Removal: Why Ambitious 'No Nonsense' Plans Are Vital to Limit Global Heating to 2°C," *The Conversation*, September 22, 2023, http://theconversation.com/carbon-removal-why-ambitious-no-nonsense-plans-are-vital-to-limit-global-heating-to-2-212462.
9. For detailed reports on each of these carbon removal projects, see "Carbon Offsets and Carbon Removals Research," Giving Green, n.d., https://www.givinggreen.earth/carbon-offsets-removals.
10. For detailed reports on each of these emission reduction projects, see "Carbon Offsets and Carbon Removals Research."
11. Lucia Simonelli and Dan Stein, "How to Think Beyond Net

Zero," Giving Green, January 2023, https://www.givinggreen.earth/carbon-offsets-research/how-to-think-beyond-net-zero.

12 For detailed reports on Frontier and Milkywire, see "Carbon Offsets and Carbon Removals Research."

13 Max Roser, "Why Did Renewables Become so Cheap so Fast?," *Our World in Data*, December 28, 2023, https://ourworldindata.org/cheap-renewables-growth.

14 Hannah Ritchie, Max Roser, and Pablo Rosado, "Renewable Energy," *Our World in Data*, January 4, 2024, https://ourworldindata.org/renewable-energy.

15 "U.S. Electric Power Generation Employment 2022," Statista, January 17, 2024, https://www.statista.com/statistics/660342/number-of-employees-in-electric-power-generation-by-technology-in-the-us/.

16 Roser, "Why Did Renewables Become so Cheap so Fast?"

17 John Halstead, "Climate Change Cause Area Report," Founders Pledge, May 2018, https://www.founderspledge.com/downloads/fp-climate-change; "CATF Cost-Effectiveness," Founders Pledge, n.d., https://docs.google.com/spreadsheets/d/1q6srpmt5VkdXLGfYzqHqkU3hvGUwPKjA67uxqYI0Upw/.

18 "2022 in Climate Change: Almost a Disaster, But Hope Prevails," *TIME*, December 26, 2022, https://time.com/6243369/2022-climate-change-recap/.

19 Johannes Ackva, Luisa Sandkühler, and Violet Buxton-Walsh, "Guide to the Changing Landscape of Climate Philanthropy," July 12, 2022, https://www.founderspledge.com/research/changing-landscape.

20 Giving Green, "Top Climate Nonprofits 2023: Best Bets for Your Climate Donation," Giving Green, November 11, 2023, https://www.givinggreen.earth/post/top-climate-nonprofits-2023-best-bets-for-your-climate-donation.

21 Giving Green, "Giving Green Fund: Why Donate to an Expertly Curated Climate Fund?," Giving Green, December 18, 2023, https://www.givinggreen.earth/post/giving-green-fund-about.

22 Giving Green, "Giving Green Grantmaking Fund," n.d., https://www.givingwhatwecan.org/charities/giving-green-fund; "Founders Pledge: Climate Change Fund," Giving What We Can, n.d., https://www.givingwhatwecan.org/charities/founders-pledge-climate-change-fund.

23 Ming Xu and Morteza Taiebat, "5 Charts Show How Your Household Drives up Global Greenhouse Gas Emissions," *The Conversation*, September 10, 2019, http://theconversation.com/5-charts-show-how-your-household-drives-up-global-greenhouse-gas-emissions-119968; Kaihui Song et al., "Scale, Distribution and Variations of Global Greenhouse Gas Emissions Driven by U.S. Households," *Environment International* 133 (December 1, 2019), 105137, https://doi.org/10.1016/j.envint.2019.105137.

24 Xu and Taiebat, "5 Charts Show How Your Household Drives up Global Greenhouse Gas Emissions"; Song et al., "Scale, Distribution and Variations of Global Greenhouse Gas Emissions Driven by U.S. Households."

25 Hannah Ritchie and Max Roser, "You Want to Reduce the Carbon Footprint of Your Food? Focus on What You Eat, Not Whether Your Food Is Local," *Our World in Data*, January 24, 2020, https://ourworldindata.org/food-choice-vs-eating-local.

26 Ritchie and Roser, "You Want to Reduce the Carbon Footprint of Your Food?"

27 Xu and Taiebat, "5 Charts Show How Your Household Drives up Global Greenhouse Gas Emissions"; Song et al., "Scale, Distribution and Variations of Global Greenhouse Gas Emissions Driven by U.S. Households."

28 Hannah Ritchie, "Which Form of Transport Has the Smallest Carbon Footprint?," *Our World in Data*, August 30, 2023, https://ourworldindata.org/travel-carbon-footprint.

29 Ritchie, "Which Form of Transport Has the Smallest Carbon Footprint?"

30 Xu and Taiebat, "5 Charts Show How Your Household Drives up Global Greenhouse Gas Emissions"; Song et al., "Scale, Distribution and Variations of Global Greenhouse Gas Emissions Driven by U.S. Households."

31 U.S. Energy Information Administration (EIA), "Use of Energy in Homes," December 18, 2023, https://www.eia.gov/energyexplained/use-of-energy/homes.php.

32 U.S. Department of Energy, "Heat Pump Systems," n.d., https://www.energy.gov/energysaver/heat-pump-systems.

33 MacAskill, *Doing Good Better*, 144.

34 Uzma Khan and Ravi Dhar, "Licensing Effect in Consumer

Choice," *Journal of Marketing Research (JMR)* 43, no. 2 (May 2006), 259–66, https://doi.org/10.1509/jmkr.43.2.259.
35 Nina Mazar and Chen-Bo Zhong, "Do Green Products Make Us Better People?," *Psychological Science* 21, no. 4 (April 1, 2010), 494–8, https://doi.org/10.1177/0956797610363538.
36 Irene Blanken, Niels van de Ven, and Marcel Zeelenberg, "A Meta-Analytic Review of Moral Licensing," *Personality and Social Psychology Bulletin* 41, no. 4 (April 1, 2015), 540–58, https://doi.org/10.1177/0146167215572134.
37 Ritchie et al., "Greenhouse Gas Emissions."
38 Lucas Chancel, "Global Carbon Inequality over 1990–2019," *Nature Sustainability* 5, no. 11 (November 2022), 931–8, https://doi.org/10.1038/s41893-022-00955-z.
39 Hannah Ritchie, "We Need the Right Kind of Climate Optimism," Vox, March 13, 2023, https://www.vox.com/the-highlight/23622511/climate-doomerism-optimism-progress-environmentalism.
40 Ritchie et al., "Greenhouse Gas Emissions."

Chapter 5: Can Your Career Save the World? Nuclear Weapons and Existential Risk

1 Benjamin Todd, *80,000 Hours: Find a Fulfilling Career That Does Good* (Oxford: Trojan House, 2023), 1.
2 For a more detailed overview of personal fit, see Benjamin Todd, "How to Find the Right Career for You," 80,000 Hours, May 2023, https://80000hours.org/career-guide/personal-fit/. For more on a related concept, comparative advantage, see Probably Good, "Comparative Advantage," n.d., https://probablygood.org/core-concepts/comparative-advantage/.
3 Todd, *80,000 Hours*, 139.
4 Todd, *80,000 Hours*, 46–54.
5 Todd, *80,000 Hours*, 106; MacAskill, *Doing Good Better*, 158.
6 Geoffrey Forden, "False Alarms on the Nuclear Front," NOVA Online PBS, October 2001, https://www.pbs.org/wgbh/nova/missileers/falsealarms.html; Ord, *The Precipice*, 96–7.
7 Paul K. Kerr and Mary Beth D. Nikitin, "Defense Primer: Command and Control of Nuclear Forces," Congressional Research Service (CRS), January 12, 2024, https://

crsreports.congress.gov/product/details?prodcode=IF10521; Jeffrey Lewis, "U.S. Presidents Are Currently Given a Four Minute Window to Decide Whether or Not to Initiate an Irreversible Apocalypse," *Foreign Policy*, August 5, 2016, https://foreignpolicy.com/2016/08/05/our-nuclear-procedures-are-crazier-than-trump/.

8   This is assuming an immediate nuclear counterstrike order. Theoretically, the president could order delayed strikes from submarines (launch-on-confirmation rather than launch-on-warning). However, immediate launch in response to an attack is likely still a prominent option. According to General Michael Hayden, former director of the CIA and NSA, the Nuclear Command and Control System is "designed for speed and decisiveness. It's not designed to debate the decision." See Kerr and Nikitin, "Defense Primer: Command and Control of Nuclear Forces."

9   Hans Kristensen et al., "Status of World Nuclear Forces," *Federation of American Scientists*, March 31, 2023, https://fas.org/initiative/status-world-nuclear-forces/.

10 Daniel Ellsberg, *The Doomsday Machine: Confessions of a Nuclear War Planner* (New York: Bloomsbury, 2017), 274.

11 Owen B. Toon et al., "Rapidly Expanding Nuclear Arsenals in Pakistan and India Portend Regional and Global Catastrophe," *Science Advances* 5, no. 10 (October 2, 2019), eaay5478, https://doi.org/10.1126/sciadv.aay5478.

12 Max Roser, "Nuclear Weapons: Why Reducing the Risk of Nuclear War Should Be a Key Concern of Our Generation," *Our World in Data*, March 3, 2022, https://ourworldindata.org/nuclear-weapons-risk.

13 Nick Bostrom, "Existential Risks: Analyzing Human Extinction Scenarios," *Journal of Evolution and Technology* 9, no. 1 (2002), https://nickbostrom.com/existential/risks.

14 Ord, *The Precipice*, 71–2.

15 Ord, *The Precipice*, 74–7.

16 Ord, *The Precipice*, 31–2.

17 Daniel Ellsberg, "Risking Doomsday: Atmospheric Ignition," in *The Doomsday Machine: Confessions of a Nuclear War Planner* (New York: Bloomsbury, 2017), 274–85.

18 Ord, *The Precipice*, 92.

19 Benjamin Todd, "The Case for Reducing Existential Risks,"

80,000 Hours, June 2022, https://80000hours.org/articles/existential-risks/. Todd combines the last two into one category, so his list, while having the same components, is condensed into three groups: 1. Targeted efforts, 2. Broad efforts, 3. Learning more and building capacity.
20 Nick Bostrom, "Existential Risk Prevention as Global Priority," *Global Policy* 4, no. 1 (February 2013), 15–31, https://doi.org/10.1111/1758-5899.12002.
21 Benjamin Todd, "Which Jobs Help People the Most?," in *80,000 Hours: Find a Fulfilling Career That Does Good* (Oxford: Trojan House, 2023), https://80000hours.org/career-guide/high-impact-jobs/. The list is slightly reworded and reordered, with the most significant change being combining earning to give within a broader category of support roles.
22 Todd, "How to Find the Right Career for You."
23 Matthew Gentzel, "It's Time for a New Atomic Altruism," *Vox*, August 4, 2023, https://www.vox.com/future-perfect/2023/8/4/23819209/nuclear-war-philanthropies-oppenheimer-united-states-china-russia-cold-war-existential-risk.
24 Ord, *The Precipice*, 167.
25 Ord, *The Precipice*, 167.
26 "36 Deadliest Tourist Activities and Adventure Sports (2023 Study)," June 26, 2023, https://www.nomadicyak.com/dangerous-adventure-sports-travel-activities/.
27 Worldometer, "World Population by Year," n.d., https://www.worldometers.info/world-population/world-population-by-year/.
28 Todd, "The Case for Reducing Existential Risks."

Chapter 6: High Risks and Rewards: AI and Longtermism
1 Ord, *The Precipice*, 167.
2 William MacAskill, "'Longtermism,'" EA Forum, July 25, 2019, https://forum.effectivealtruism.org/posts/qZyshHCNkjs3TvSem/longtermism.
3 William MacAskill, "Longtermism," n.d., https://www.williammacaskill.com/longtermism.
4 For example, here are some quotes from Thunberg's speeches: "You say you love your children above all else and yet you're stealing their future in front of their very eyes" (UN Climate Conference 2018); "Our house is on fire. I am here to say our

house is on fire … I want you to act as if the house was on fire, because it is" (World Economic Forum 2019); "You have stolen my dreams and my childhood with your empty words … The eyes of all future generations are upon you" (UN Climate Summit 2019). For full transcripts of Thunberg's speeches, see Phil Stubbs, "Greta Thunberg Quotes," *The Environment Show* (blog), April 7, 2020, https://www.environmentshow.com/greta-thunberg-quotes/.

5 For more on these concepts, see Ibo van de Poel and Lambèr Royakkers, "Sustainability, Ethics, and Technology," in *Ethics, Technology, and Engineering: An Introduction*, 2nd ed. (Hoboken, NJ: Wiley Blackwell, 2023), 246–51.

6 William MacAskill, "The Case for Longtermism," *The New York Times*, August 5, 2022, sec. Opinion, https://www.nytimes.com/2022/08/05/opinion/the-case-for-longtermism.html.

7 Worldometer, "World Population by Year."

8 "World City Populations 2024," n.d., https://worldpopulationreview.com/world-cities.

9 Hannah Ritchie et al., "Five Key Findings from the 2022 UN Population Prospects," Our World in Data, July 11, 2022, https://ourworldindata.org/world-population-update-2022.

10 This is meant as an illustration, not a prediction. With a life expectancy of 82 (this is what the UN projects for 2100), at least 10 billion people would need to be born every 82 years to maintain a stable population, which is around 122 million per year. So, over 1,000 years, 122 billion people would be born. According to Our World in Data, around 109 billion people have died. Adding our current population of around 8 billion, that brings us to around 117 billion people born over the past 200–300,000 years, compared to 122 billion who could be born over the next 1,000 years (author's calculations). To see estimates of population over the next 800,000 years and more, see Max Roser, "The Future Is Vast: What Does This Mean for Our Own Life?," *Our World in Data*, December 28, 2023, https://ourworldindata.org/the-future-is-vast. For more on population and life expectancy estimates, see United Nations, Department of Economic and Social Affairs, Population Division, "World Population Prospects," 2022, https://population.un.org/wpp/.

11 Using the concept of complementary probability, if the probability of not having an existential catastrophe over the next

100 years is 5/6, and it remains the same for each century after that, over a 1,000-year time period, the odds of avoiding an existential catastrophe would be only $(5/6)^{10}$, approximately 16.15%; in this case, the probability of an existential catastrophe occurring over the next 1,000 years would be around 83.85% (1 − 0.1615).

12 Katja Grace et al., "Thousands of AI Authors on the Future of AI," AI Impacts, January 4, 2024, https://aiimpacts.org/research-reports/.
13 For more discussion on the definition and forms of superintelligence, see Nick Bostrom, "Forms of Superintelligence," in *Superintelligence: Paths, Dangers, Strategies* (Oxford: Oxford University Press, 2017), Ch. 6.
14 Nick Bostrom, "Ethical Issues in Advanced Artificial Intelligence," in *Cognitive, Emotive and Ethical Aspects of Decision Making in Humans and in Artificial Intelligence* 2, no. I (2003), 12–17.
15 Holden Karnofsky, "AI Could Defeat All Of Us Combined," Cold Takes, June 9, 2022, https://www.cold-takes.com/ai-could-defeat-all-of-us-combined/.
16 "Pause Giant AI Experiments: An Open Letter," Future of Life Institute, March 22, 2023, https://futureoflife.org/open-letter/pause-giant-ai-experiments/; Ryan Browne, "Elon Musk and Other Tech Leaders Call for Pause on 'Dangerous Race' to Make A.I. as Advanced as Humans," CNBC, March 29, 2023, https://www.cnbc.com/2023/03/29/elon-musk-other-tech-leaders-pause-training-ai-beyond-gpt-4.html.
17 Bostrom, "Ethical Issues in Advanced Artificial Intelligence."
18 MacAskill, *What We Owe the Future*, 226–7. For an excellent summary of the book, see Fin Moorhouse, "Summary of What We Owe The Future," January 20, 2023, https://finmoorhouse.com/writing/wwotf-summary/.
19 For more suggestions see the section titled "What are the best ways to help future generations right now?" in Cody Fenwick, "Longtermism: A Call to Protect Future Generations," 80,000 Hours, March 2023, https://80000hours.org/articles/future-generations/.
20 Benjamin Hilton, "Preventing an AI-Related Catastrophe: Problem Profile," 80,000 Hours, March 2023, https://80000hours.org/problem-profiles/artificial-intelligence/.

21 "Statement on AI Risk," Center for AI Safety, n.d., https://www.safe.ai/statement-on-ai-risk; Kevin Roose, "A.I. Poses 'Risk of Extinction,' Industry Leaders Warn," *The New York Times*, May 30, 2023, sec. Technology, https://www.nytimes.com/2023/05/30/technology/ai-threat-warning.html.

Chapter 7: Making a Difference through Effective Altruism

1 Charity Entrepreneurship, "Track Record," n.d., https://www.charityentrepreneurship.com/our-charities.
2 UNESCO Institute for Statistics, "Literacy," n.d., https://uis.unesco.org/en/topic/literacy.
3 This report estimated that 6.7% of the world has a college degree in 2010, up from 5.9% in 2000. If similar growth trends held, that would put 2020 at around 7.5%. Robert J. Barro and Jong-Wha Lee, "A New Data Set of Educational Attainment in the World, 1950-2010," *NBER Working Papers*, April 2010, https://ideas.repec.org/p/nbr/nberwo/15902.html.
4 US Census Bureau, "CPS Historical Time Series Visualizations," Census.gov, February 14, 2022, https://www.census.gov/library/visualizations/time-series/demo/cps-historical-time-series.html.
5 Author's estimate. Globally speaking, very few people have heard of effective altruism, let alone know much about the movement's ideas and organizations. For example, according to a 2022 survey, only 2.6–6.7% of adults in the USA have even heard of effective altruism. David Moss and Jamie Elsey, "How Many People Have Heard of Effective Altruism?," Rethink Priorities, May 20, 2022, https://rethinkpriorities.org/publications/how-many-people-have-heard-of-effective-altruism.
6 See Chapter 2, section 2.1.
7 Domenico Montanaro, "Poll: Despite Record Turnout, 80 Million Americans Didn't Vote. Here's Why," *NPR*, December 15, 2020, sec. Politics, https://www.npr.org/2020/12/15/945031391/poll-despite-record-turnout-80-million-americans-didnt-vote-heres-why; Kelly Devine, "Visualizing Voter Turnout in Local and School Board Elections," *Carnegie Reporter*, November 2, 2022, https://www.carnegie.org/our-work/article/visualizing-voter-turnout-local-school-board-elections/.

8 MacAskill, *Doing Good Better*, 109.
9 Michael Townsend and Sjir Hoeijmakers, "Why We Recommend Using Expert-Led Charitable Funds," Giving What We Can, November 14, 2022, https://www.givingwhatwecan.org/why-we-recommend-funds; GiveWell, "Our Giving Funds"; The Life You Can Save, "Cause Funds," n.d., https://www.thelifeyoucansave.org/cause-funds/.
10 MacAskill, *Doing Good Better*, 201–2.
11 Upcoming events can be found at "Effective Altruism Global | Effective Altruism," n.d., https://www.effectivealtruism.org/ea-global.

Index

80,000 Hours, 46, 57, 87, 113–15, 122, 124, 128, 133–4, 178, 185

abortion, 63
accelerationism, 157
advocacy, 4, 57, 82–3, 95, 97–9, 163, 176–7
  see also SDAC framework
Against Malaria Foundation, 36–7
AI (artificial intelligence), 5, 19, 58, 120, 130, 138–9, 140, 149–65
  alignment problem, 154, 157, 158, 163
  consciousness, 158–9
  interpretability problem, 152, 157
  safety research, 155, 157, 163
  see also generative AI
air-conditioning, 103–4
algorithmic bias, 160
altruistic superpowers, 170–3, 186

animal charities, 83, 169, 176
Animal Charity Evaluators, 83, 169, 176
animal rights, 68, 71
animal welfare, 4, 18–20, 58, 61, 64–83, 134, 176, 178, 179
anthropocentrism, 65–6, 71, 77–8
anthropogenic risks, 119, 120–2, 140–3
antimalarial drugs, 36
artificial general intelligence (AGI), 150–1, 154–5, 158
artificial intelligence (AI), *see* AI (artificial intelligence)
artificial narrow intelligence (ANI), 149
artificial superintelligence (ASI), 150–5, 156, 158
asteroid impacts, 119, 140, 143
automation, 160
autonomous weapons, 160
awareness, 15, 25, 101, 109, 125, 129, 163, 177

Bankman-Fried, Sam, 45–6
bed-nets, 36–7
Biden, Joe, 164
biochar, 92
biomass carbon removal and storage, 92
biosecurity, 15, 17, 25, 162
biotechnology, 120, 139
Black Death, 130
blindness, 4, 16, 30, 35
Bostrom, Nick, 118, 123, 134, 140, 141–2, 150–5, 156–7
broad-scope efforts, 122–3
BURN, 93
burnout, 9, 49, 51
Bykvist, Krister, 69

capacity building, 123, 133
carbon capture *see* carbon removal
carbon footprints, 77–8, 89, 91, 94, 95, 100–6, 174
carbon neutrality, 91, 94, 95
carbon offset registries, 90–1
carbon offsets, 88–95, 100
carbon removal, 92–3, 94
carbon sequestration, 89–90, 92
Carbon180, 99
careers
  career capital, 114–15
  career satisfaction, 57, 114, 128
  in the charity sector, 43, 44, 57, 126
  in the communications sector, 5, 114, 124, 125–6
  earning to give, 31, 41–4, 45–7, 57, 113, 124, 126–7, 133
  evaluating career impact, 114
  in the finance sector, 45–6
  governmental policy work, 5, 114, 124–5, 133
  high-impact, 4–5, 112–15, 124–34, 177–8, 185
  high-paying, 41–4, 45–7, 57, 113
  organization building, 5, 114, 124, 126
  potentially harmful careers, 45–7, 115, 178
  in the research sector, 5, 114, 124, 125, 133, 163
  see also SDAC framework
Carnegie Endowment of International Peace, 123
catalytic carbon removal portfolios, 94
catastrophic risks *see* existential risks
Center for AI Safety, 164
Centers for Disease Control and Prevention (CDC), 15
Centre for the Study of Existential Risk, 134
certification, 90–1
charities
  animal charities, 83, 169, 176
  careers with, 43, 44, 57, 126
  climate charities, 98, 100, 176
  cost-effectiveness, 4, 30, 36–7, 43–4, 98, 175
  evaluation of, 4, 30, 34–8, 47–8, 58, 83, 98, 169, 175–6
  high-impact, 4, 30, 34–8, 43–4, 58, 113, 169, 175–6, 185

Index

potential negative impacts of, 47–8, 175
volunteering for, 54, 113
Charity Entrepreneurship, 126, 169
Charm Industrial, 92
ChatGPT, 150, 154, 155, 156, 163–4
child mortality, 30, 31–2, 36, 37, 54–5, 141
China, 56, 65, 117
Clean Air Task Force, 98, 99
Climate Bill (US, 2022), 98–9, 108
climate change, 4, 19, 58, 87–109, 120, 134, 139, 140, 144, 148, 156, 162, 176
climate charities *see* charities, climate
climate defeatism, 107–8
Climate Transformation Fund, 94
Climeworks, 92
Cold War, 4, 115–16
communications careers, 5, 114, 124, 125–6
communities of givers, 49–50, 183–4
consciousness, 159
consumer spending, 48–9
cooking stoves, 93
Corporate Accountability, 90
cost-effectiveness, 4, 30, 36–7, 43–4, 91, 94, 98, 99, 131–2, 159, 175, 180
counterfactual thinking, 43, 169, 181
counterterrorism, 13–14
COVID-19 pandemic, 3, 7–11, 15, 16–17, 24, 26

criminal justice reform, 19, 63
cryptocurrency, 45–6
cybersecurity, 160

data-driven safe-bets approach, 81
decision-making, 5, 19, 82
deep fakes, 160
democracy, 19, 171–2
deterrence, 117
diminishing returns, law of, 14
direct cash transfers, 4, 36
discrimination, 20, 62, 67
diseases, 4, 15, 30, 56, 139
  see also pandemics
disjunctive worry, 62–3
diversified portfolio approach, 80–1
diversity, 162
donation amounts, 49–53
  see also SDAC framework
drinking water, 35, 47

earning to give, 31, 41–4, 45–7, 57, 113, 124, 126–7, 133
economic development, 56
economies, potential harms to, 48–9
education, 31, 170–1
electric vehicles, 103
Effective Altruism Forum, 183–4
"Effective Altruism Global" conferences, 184
Effective Ventures, 176
Ellsberg, Daniel, 117
emissions reduction programs, 89, 93–4
energy efficiency, 93, 104, 105–6

energy production, 89, 95–7, 139, 148
energy, renewable *see* renewable energy
energy, wind *see* wind energy
engineered pandemics, 17, 120, 122, 130, 140, 156
  see also pandemics
equal consideration principle, 67
ethics, 22, 42, 63–4, 69
European Union, 32, 117
Evidence Action, 35
existential risks, 4, 18–20, 58, 112, 118–35, 138, 140–3, 148–9, 151–61, 164, 176, 179
expected value theory, 4, 61, 72–82, 169
extinctions *see* human extinction; mass extinction events; species extinction
extreme weather events, 4, 106

factory farming, 4, 19, 58, 61, 64–8, 75–7, 82–3, 174
Faunalytics, 83
Fermi estimates, 81
finance careers, 45–6
fishing, 79
forests, 89, 90–1
Fortify Health, 169
fossil fuels, 139, 141
Founders Pledge, 87, 98, 99, 169, 176
France, 117
Fred Hollows Foundation, 35
Freeman, Luke, 51–2
Frontier, 94
FTX, 45–6
  see also Bankman-Fried, Sam

future generations, 5, 23, 62–3, 119, 121, 132, 138–49, 158, 160–5
Future of Life Institute, 123, 134, 155, 164

gain-of-function (GOF) research, 25
gambling, 73–4
general intelligence, 149–50
generative AI, 150, 152, 155, 160
generosity, 52
genocide, 62
GHG emissions *see* greenhouse gas (GHG) emissions
GiveDirectly, 36
GiveWell, 35, 36, 37, 44, 47, 48, 155, 169, 176
giving
  all-or-nothing, 51
  evidence-based, 35
  global, 53–6
  high-impact charitable, 3, 4, 43–4, 54, 57
  hits-based approaches, 80
  local, 53–4
  as a moral duty, 41, 44
  objections to, 45–9, 57
  pledges, 50, 51, 52, 185
  standards, 51–2
giving funds, 48, 99, 176
Giving Green, 87, 91–5, 97, 99, 169, 176
Giving What We Can, 34–5, 36, 41, 48, 49–52, 58, 127, 169, 176, 185
Global Priorities Institute, 22
global priorities research, 20, 22, 123

Index

Good Energy Collective, 99
Good Food Institute, 83, 99
governmental policy work, 5, 114, 124–5, 133
green technologies, 4, 94, 95–7, 99, 108
greenhouse gas (GHG) emissions, 78, 93, 88–109
Guardian, 90

habitat destruction, 19, 76, 153
Hassenfeld, Elie, 35
heat pumps, 104
heating, 103–4, 106
Helen Keller International, 37
high-impact careers *see* careers, high-impact
high-impact charities *see* charities, high-impact
high-paying careers *see* careers, high-paying
high-risk, high-reward strategies, 80–1
Hilton, Benjamin, 163
home energy use, 101, 103–4, 105–6
hospital admission, 8–10
human extinction, 118–19, 129, 131, 132, 140–3, 148, 153, 158
human resilience, 130–1
Humane League, 83
Hutchinson, Michelle, 3

income distribution, 32–4, 171
incommensurable goods, 22
India, 56, 117, 118
inductive worry, 62
Industrious Labs, 99
innovation, 4, 57, 94–7, 99, 120–1, 139–43, 147–8, 154, 164–5
instrumental value, 66
insulation, 104
intergenerational justice, 144–5
International Peace Museum, 123
intrinsic value, 66–7
investigative approaches, 123–4, 133
iodine deficiency, 35
Iodine Global Network, 35
Israel, 117

John Hopkins Center for Health Security, 25

Karnofsky, Holden, 35, 155, 157

lab leaks, 17, 25, 120
launch on warning strategy, 116
law of large numbers, 73
Lead Exposure Elimination Project, 169
leakage, 89, 90
Life You Can Save, The, 169, 176, 185
lifestyle changes, 87, 100–7, 174–5
see also SDAC framework
lighting, 103, 105–6
living standards, 32, 49, 51–2
longtermism, 5, 23, 134, 138–9, 143–9, 158–61, 164
Longview Philanthropy, 176
local food production, 101–2
Lovely, Garrison, 78–9

low-hanging fruit, 14, 174
Lusk, Jayson, 75

MacArthur Foundation, 129
MacAskill, William, 3, 34–5, 41–4, 50, 69, 71–2, 104, 113, 144, 145, 147, 161–3, 175, 179
making a difference, 30, 43, 114, 168–86
malaria, 36–7
Malaria Consortium, 36
managed giving funds, 48, 99, 176
Manhattan Project, 121
Marris, Emma, 22
MASH Makes, 92
mass extinction events, 119, 143
maximize expected choice-worthiness (MEC) approach, 61, 70–2
meat
 alternatives, 19, 83
 consumption, 4, 19, 65, 74–8, 78–9, 101, 105, 174
 production, 4, 19, 25, 61, 64–8, 74–8, 82–3, 101, 174
 see also factory farming; veganism
medical care, access to, 4, 18, 31
medical triage, 7–11, 23–4
mental health, 19, 74
methane, 88, 90
Milkywire, 94
misinformation, 126, 160, 178
moonshot investing, 80

moral blind spots, 62, 158
moral catastrophes, 62–8, 158
moral caution, 46, 70–2, 78, 169, 182
moral disagreement, 69
moral licensing, 87, 104–7, 175
moral obligation, 30–1, 38–41, 50–1, 144–6
moral uncertainty, 4, 46, 61, 68–72, 169
moral weights, 66, 76–7, 82
Morgan, Holly, 3
mutually assured destruction (MAD), 116–17
my favorite theory (MFT) approach, 69–71

natural disasters, 56
natural risks, 119–20, 140, 143
neartermism, 23, 139, 158–61
neglectedness, 3, 7, 11–18, 21, 23, 26, 114, 126, 128–9, 169, 174, 179–81
 see also SNS framework
net-zero carbon *see* carbon neutrality
New Incentives, 37
New Zealand, 129–30
Nigeria, 37
nitrous oxide, 88
non-additionality, 89, 90
non-permanence, 89–90
North Korea, 117
Norwood, Bailey, 75
novel pathogens, 25
Nuclear Age Peace Foundation, 123
nuclear energy, 139
Nuclear Threat Initiative, 123
nuclear weapons, 4–5, 19, 58,

112, 115–35, 139, 140, 142, 144, 156
nuclear winter, 4, 118, 129–30, 143
nutrition, 18, 31, 56, 169

OpenAI, 150
Open Philanthropy, 155
opportunity, 172–3
Opportunity Green, 99
optimistic changemakers, 108
Ord, Toby, 3, 34–5, 41, 50, 69, 120–1, 129–30, 140, 144, 148, 161
organization building, 5, 114, 124, 126
Our World in Data, 118
overconfidence, 69, 182
overlooked issues, 20, 21–2, 80

Pakistan, 117, 118
pandemics, 7–11, 12, 64, 130, 156
  pandemic prevention, 3, 15–17, 24–6, 58
  see also COVID-19 pandemic; engineered pandemics; vaccines
paperclip maximizer thought experiment, 153
pathogen detection, 16
pathogen research, 25, 120, 139
personal fit, 17–18, 114, 128
personal protective equipment, 10
pescatarianism, 78–9
Petrov, Stanislav, 115–16, 118
phantom offsets, 91
PlayPumps, 47

pledges, public giving, 50, 52, 127, 185
  see also Giving What We Can; Founders Pledge
policy advocacy, 4, 57, 82–3, 95, 97–9, 163, 177
political influence, 171–2
pond analogy, 38–41, 51, 52
population growth, 145–7
poverty, 4, 18–20, 30–58, 64, 131, 134, 144, 157, 169, 179
PREDICT program, 15
primates, 152
prioritization, 3, 5, 7–11, 20–4, 26, 123, 158–61
Probably Good, 133–4, 178, 185
problem, scale of, 11–12
Project InnerSpace, 99
proxy wars, 117
public transport, 103

quantification bias, 21–2
quantification problems, 81

racism, 62, 67
refrigeration, 103
Regan, Tom, 67, 68
regulation, 19, 82–3, 97, 142, 155, 163
renewable energy, 89, 95–7, 104, 148, 162
research careers, 5, 114, 124, 125, 133, 163
resilience, 130–1
resource scarcity, 8, 10
Rethink Priorities, 22
risk reduction, 4, 5, 19, 58, 112, 122–34, 140–3, 148–9, 156–61, 164, 176, 179

risks *see* anthropogenic risks; existential risks; natural risks
Risks and Resilience Fund, 127
Ritchie, Hannah, 101, 108
Roman civilization, 62
Russia, 117, 129
  see also Soviet Union

sanitation, 18, 31
scale, 3, 7, 11–18, 21, 23, 26, 114, 133, 169, 174, 179–81
  see also SNS framework
scale, neglectedness, and solvability (SNS) framework *see* SNS framework
scarcity *see* resource scarcity
SDAC framework, 173–9
sentiocentrism, 66–8, 71
sexism, 62, 67
Singer, Peter, 37–41, 48, 50–1, 52–3, 67, 68
slavery, 62
SNS framework, 3, 7, 11–18, 20–4, 26, 114, 169, 174, 179–81
solar energy, 95–7, 104, 148
solvability, 3, 7, 11–18, 21, 23, 26, 114, 133, 169, 174, 179–81
  see also SNS framework
Soviet Union, 115–16
  see also Russia
species extinction, 22, 119–20, 143
speciesism, 67
standstill principle, 145

Stanford Existential Risk Initiative, 134
super-volcanoes, 119–20, 140
supporting roles, 124, 126–7
sustainable development, 145
systemic change, 4, 87, 95–100, 106, 108–9, 177

targeted efforts, 122
technology, 4, 54, 94–7, 99, 108, 120–1, 123, 131, 134–5, 138–43, 147–65
Temkin, Larry, 47
TerraPraxis, 99
terrorism, 12–14
Thunberg, Greta, 144
time capsule thought experiment, 146
Todd, Benjamin, 3, 113, 122, 124, 128
total travel miles, 102–3
Tradewater, 93
transportation, 100, 101, 102–3
  see also carbon footprints
triage, 7–11, 23–4
Trinity Test, 121

Ukraine, 117, 129
uncertainty, 4, 22–4, 46, 58, 61, 68–72, 81–3, 130–3, 160, 161–2, 181–2
unintended consequences, 5, 45, 120, 152–3
United Kingdom, 117, 164
United States, 13–15, 24, 32–3, 64, 74, 77, 97–9, 106, 108, 115–17, 129, 164, 170–2
urn of invention, 141–2

Index

vaccines, 10, 16, 37, 139
veganism, 61, 71–2, 74–8, 178
vitamin A deficiency, 37
volunteering, 54, 113, 180

warfare, 4–5, 19, 24, 56, 112, 115–35, 140, 142, 144, 156
warming effects, 88

water
  heating, 103–4
  supply, 35, 47
wealth, 31–4, 52, 171
Wild Animal Initiative, 83
wild animals, 19, 25, 83
Williams, Evan G., 62–4
wind energy, 89, 95–7, 148